Survival of the European (Dis) Union

John Theodore

Survival of the European (Dis) Union

Responses to Populism, Nativism and Globalization

palgrave
macmillan

John Theodore
Manchester, UK

ISBN 978-3-030-31213-8 ISBN 978-3-030-31214-5 (eBook)
https://doi.org/10.1007/978-3-030-31214-5

This Palgrave Macmillan imprint is published by the registered company Springer Nature Switzerland AG
The registered company address is: Gewerbestrasse 11, 6330 Cham, Switzerland

Foreword

The European Union has transfixed and divided the right of British politics for a generation—a virus that has now infected the whole nation with the narrow Leave victory in the 2016 referendum. The EU is the talismanic bogeyman that has propelled the rise of Nigel Farage, his UKIP and now his Brexit party and in response forced a broad church Conservative party to transmute into a narrow right-wing English nationalist sect. It has exposed the unwritten British constitution as too weak a vessel to manage and contain the intense tensions aroused by trying to fashion an exit from the EU that is not self-defeatingly painful. Beyond all of that, there is the prospect of leaving the EU without any form of deal—becoming a third country sundering the multiple relationships built up over 42 years and triggering a major recession. How did it ever come to this?

The EU has been portrayed by the British right as something it is not—a triumph of crooked ideology in search of enemies to justify itself over reality. As this book explains, it is not an aspirant superstate robbing its members of political autonomy, locking them in a Brussels devised straightjacket. It is not the locus of a suffocating regulation that muzzles entrepreneurship. Nor is it the cause of every demon that haunts the white working class, especially immigration. Rather it is a club of countries with similar values and aspirations that attempts to ensure peace, trade, openness and prosperity in our shared continent and for all its members creates the collective capacity to secure their interests before the challenge of the USA and China.

Britain, far from being the victim of a continental plot, has benefited enormously from membership—fashioning rules that have become global standards, attracting enormous inward investment, establishing the City of London as the centre of global finance and raising standards for the environment and in work.

In fact, the EU has partially mitigated the failings of our political class in creating an economic model that works for all—yet the right has brilliantly pinned the blame for failings made at home in Europe. The EU has replaced nationalized industries and trade unions as the imagined new threat; rather than thinking through a positive way forward, it would rather blame the foreigner, the other, the European.

This book sets out to dismantle the bogeyman and replace it with a more rounded vision of the EU, acknowledging its weaknesses while calmly and rationally stressing the nobility of its aims. It is long overdue. Brexit is but a more extreme example of forces that are rocking the EU to its foundations. Everywhere in Europe, there is a sense that international co-operation is ineffective and that living standards are under pressure—from immigration, from globalization and from technological change—that only strong leaders in strong nation states acting only in their own interests can solve. The EU is ineffective and besides the point.

Before this assault, European citizens of whatever political hue need the centre to hold—and the EU badly needs to get better at delivering tangible benefits to embolden them to stand by it. It is an existential battle. In Britain, we too need to recognize that the EU is a force for good and stand by it. John Theodore has done that cause a great service in this timely and carefully argued book—including advice to the EU as much to its British readers. Nobody knows how this story will end in the immediate future. But eventually, as Theodore argues, there will have to be an EU working better than it does today. The task is to do it—and this book is a valuable contribution to making that future happen.

Will Hutton
Principal of Hertford College Oxford University
London, UK

Preface

My argument in this book is that, despite its many shortcomings, the European project still has every chance—and every need—to survive. But this will only be the case if it learns the hard lessons from the crises and drama that have plunged much of the continent into social, economic and political turmoil.

The EU is increasingly perceived as an entity its founders never intended for it: a superstate, ossified and out of touch at best, and corrupt and tyrannical at worst. This image, as I will demonstrate in detail, is wildly mistaken. But it is one that has been seized on by populists of both the extreme Left and Right, with devastating political consequences: consequences seen in everything from Brexit to the rise of SYRIZA and Golden Dawn and other populist movements in Eastern Europe. Such parties, increasingly, have grasped the pulse of popular opinion, on issues ranging from political integration to mass migration and austerity economics.

But the narrative is still a false one. The EU is not a superstate; and, though its institutions have many flaws, the alternatives to this system being put forward by its opponents will be far worse. The EU needs reform, not revolution. The rising tide of nationalism, nativism and politically polarized tribalism are palliatives for the popular mood—not the foundation for any real and lasting alternative. Much like previous phases of social and economic trauma, the crises on the continent since 2008 open up a real space for renewal and reform. The only question now is will the right lessons be learnt. This book will be a major contribution to this discussion. My take on this topic is unique, and based on my experiences as professional practitioner, twice-published writer, and public speaker on the subject. I have directed practical multi-partnered EU projects, produced two recent books that explored major issues in Europe, particularly Brexit and austerity economics, and spoken repeatedly at the European Parliament. I guest—lectured at 'European Cities Week' in the Committee for the Regions. I was interviewed on BBC Radio and BBC TV north on immigration issues and on TV Krakow in Poland on cross-border EU projects.

I have been researching European matters and international affairs since the 1970s. Recently, I have published two books entitled: *Cyprus and the Financial Crisis the Controversial Bailout* (Palgrave: 2015) and *The European Union and the Eurozone Under Stress* (Palgrave: 2017) and over 30 articles on European Affairs, which have received acclaim for their research and analysis. These include high profile interviews with top players in government, academia and European affairs—many of whom revealed things to me that they did not disclose elsewhere. My network of contacts in Britain and Europe is extensive, has been built over decades, and stretches across governments and private institutions.

While passionate about the EU, I remain a fierce critic of its failings and undemocratic powers. But I will explain that giving voice to peoples' frustrations is one thing—providing real answers quite another. Populism in its different forms has become a convenient tool for autocrats and would-be demagogues. It has become their pretext to muzzle the media, erode free speech, threaten the rule of law and endanger the fabric of the civic society. Recent events in Hungary and Poland are merely the tip of this ominous iceberg. And isolationist trends and populist shocks in the United States threatening the multilateral order on which the EU depends.

Manchester, UK John Theodore

Acknowledgements

I would like to express my deep thanks to all those who have kindly given me their valuable time in helping to record the events, especially Jonathan my son for his editorial help throughout and to Dr. Dimitrios Syrrakos for his specialist advice and guidance on the latest developments on the Euro and the Eurozone.

My sincere gratitude is also extended to Dr. Will Hutton, the Principal of Hertford College Oxford, and Jill Evans MEP Plaid Cymru, George Shishkov, Anna Mikhailova and Hristiana Georgieva, for their views and reflections on the latest EU developments insightful observations that have helped in the writing of this book.

Finally, my thanks go to my wife Barbara for all her patience in the critical period prior to producing the manuscript and to the many EU citizens in the UK and in Europe providing their insights into the political dramas facing both the UK and Europe at present.

Timeline of the European Union

The Treaty of Rome 1957

This established the European Economic Community (EEC). The Treaty came into force in 1958. It also established the European Atomic Energy Community (Euratom).

1973: The Treaty of Accession, bringing the UK, Ireland and Denmark into the EEC.

1979: The establishment of the European Monetary System (EMS), Including the Exchange Rate Mechanism.

1979: The European Parliament was established.

1981: Greece joined the EEC.

1986: Spain and Portugal joined the EEC.

1986: The Single European Act was signed coming into force in 1987.

1990: West and East Germany reunified, bringing East Germany into the EEC.

1990: Stage 1 of European Monetary Union (EMU) began, with the removal of all restrictions on capital movements. (The UK had removed exchange controls in October 1979.)

1990: The UK joined the Exchange Rate Mechanism.

1993: The Treaty of Maastricht was ratified.

1994: Stage 2 of European Monetary Union (EMU) began, creating the advisory European Monetary Institute, followed by the launch of the European System of Central Banks. Monetary Policy.

1995: Austria, Sweden and Finland joined the EU, under the Treaty of Corfu (signed in 1994).

1997: Stability and Growth Pact signed.

1997: The Treaty of Amsterdam was signed coming into force in 1999.

1999: Stage 3 of EMU began, with the creation of the Euro and the locking-in of 11 countries states exchange rates.

2001: The Treaty of Nice was signed and came into force 2003.

2002: The Euro replaced member states' own currencies with euro notes and coins introduced.

2004: The Accession Treaty entered into force and the EU enlarged to include 10 new member states: Cyprus, the Czech Republic, Estonia, Hungary, Latvia, Lithuania, Malta, Poland, Slovakia and Slovenia.

2007: Romania and Bulgaria join the EU, taking membership to 27 states.

2007: Treaty of Lisbon signed on 13 December 2007 and came into force on 1 December 2009.

2008: Collapse of Lehman Brothers and the global financial crisis.

2010: European Financial Stability Facility (EFSF) replaced by the European Stability Mechanism (ESM).

2010: The first Greek bailout.

2013: Croatia joins the EU on 1 July as the 28th member.

2013: Ireland exits the bailout programme.

2016: Cyprus exits its bailout programme.

2016: UK Referendum 23 June resulting in a vote to leave the EU.

2018: Official date for the UK to leave the EU (March 29).

2018: EU–UK Withdrawal Agreement—unratified by the UK Parliament (14 November).

2018: Greece ends nearly 10 years of Bailouts (20 August 2018).

2019: EU Parliamentary Elections (23 May).

2019: New EU Commission President appointed (16 July).

2019: Rescheduled date for UK to leave the EU (31 October 2019).

Contents

1	**A Hierarchy of Threats**	1
	Historical Context	3
	Founding Aims	7
	Objectives of the EU	7
	The Long-Awaited Battle for the Soul of Europe	9
	The New EU Parliamentary Session	11
	Actions to Revive the European Project	13
	The New EU Parliament—Populism	15
	How the New European Parliament Will Be Different	18
	Is the USA an Existential Threat?	19
	External Threats to the EU Project	21
2	**The Survival of the Euro?**	23
	The Survival of the Euro: "Whatever It Takes"	23
	Germany and EMU	25
	Greece and the Default Threat from Italy	27
	Default Threat from Italy	30
	Efforts to Confront Weakness in the Eurozone	33

Is the Euro a Bulwark Against the Dollar? The Euro—A Weapon to Enhance Global Power 37
The Current International Role of the Euro 37
US and Iran Sanctions—Implications for the EU 39
The Euro as a Reserve Currency 41
The EU Economy 43

3 Immigration: What Now? 47
Migration—History of *Intra*-EU Mobility 47
Freedom of Movement (FOM) and Fears Raised in the UK Referendum Campaign 50
Freedom of Movement—Protecting the Rights of EU Citizens 54
The New Immigration Regime—Search for Skilled Workers 54
UK Expatriates—To What Extent Are Their Rights Preserved Post-Brexit 56
Non-EU Migration: The Search for a Solution 58
Causes of Non-EU Migration 58
Opposition to Brussels Imposed Refugee Quotas 61
Terrorism and Security Issues 62
Stemming the Flow of Non-EU Migrants Status of the EU–Turkey Agreement 64
Realpolitik in EU Foreign Relations—Negotiating with Autocratic Regimes in the Middle East 68
EU—Dialogue with the Arab League Summit 2019 70

4 Populism 73
Populism and the Redrawing of the Political Map of Europe 73
Right-Wing Populism 73
Populism in the USA 76
The Brexit Effect—And Its Effect on the EU and Eurosceptic Movements 79
Anglo-Saxon Euroscepticism 82

The Fight Back Against Populism and Authoritarianism in Eastern Europe 84
Opposition in Poland 85

5 **The EU's Illiberal Democracies** 89
Introduction 89
The Clash with Europe's Illiberal Democracies 89
Article 7 Procedure 94
Poland's March Towards Illiberalism and Autocratic Rule 97
Brussels Fights Back 98
Loss of Revenue 100
Poland's Importance to the EU After Brexit 100

6 **The EU, China and Their Changing Relations** 103
EU–China—Commercial Relations 103
Strategic Concerns 106
Chinese Investment in the Eurozone 108
Security Issues 111
How Much Is China Is Investing in the EU? 116
Approach to New Deals 118
China and the EU Without Britain 120
China's Reserve Currency Status 122

7 **Reinvigorating the EU Project** 125
"Ever Closer Union" 129
Ursula von der Leyen—A New Agenda 130
Multilateralism—EU Relations with China and the USA 132
G7 and Big Tech 137
The EU—Taxing Big Tech 138

8 **Conclusion** 149
Closer Integration 152
Lessons of Brexit 153

The Road to Democracy 153
Demands for Change 157
Recommendations for the Future 159
Benefits for EU Citizens 160

Bibliography 165

Index 173

1
A Hierarchy of Threats

Its current threats; historical and founding principles; reviving the European project; the EU parliamentary May 2019 elections; External and existential threats.

Undoubtedly, the EU and the Eurozone are in crisis. Both EU institutions and national governments are failing "the people". Enforced Brussels quotas for taking refugees have inflamed public opinion. The austerity programme inflicted on the debt-plagued countries of the Mediterranean after the 2008 global financial crisis was brutal, ineffective and inflamed public anger. It is not surprising, then, that liberal democracy—the dominant political force in Europe since the Second World War—is now reduced to fighting a rear-guard action, with its pressures and enemies continuing to mount. Nationalist-populist governments are now in power in Italy, Hungary, Poland and (through a coalition government) in Austria. The far-right party has also performed strongly in elections in France, Germany and the Netherlands and is making important gains in Spain.

J. Theodore, *Survival of the European (Dis) Union*,
https://doi.org/10.1007/978-3-030-31214-5_1

Soon after 2016, UK referendum warnings came from some key international leaders in the economic—liberalist camp each counselling Brussels to address the plight of those "left behind" by globalization. Mario Draghi, President of the European Central Bank (ECB), was one of the first to warn Brussels to pay more attention to wealth redistribution and address the concerns of consumers angered by economic inequality and job insecurity which has played into the hands of "populist" Eurosceptic parties' across the EU spectrum.

"I do not think there will be significant progress in terms of opening up markets and competition if Europe does not listen to the demands of those left behind by a society built on the pursuit of wealth and power; if Europe, as well as being a catalyst for integration and an arbiter of its rules, does not also moderate its outcomes", he said at an awards ceremony in Trento, Italy.

Draghi's warnings were echoed by Donald Tusk, President of the EU Council when he reiterated similar fears in a letter to EU leaders, saying voters wanted to know political elites were "capable of restoring control over events and processes which overwhelm, disorientate and sometimes terrify them". "History has taught us that this [discontent] can lead to a massive turn away from freedom and other fundamental values that the EU is founded upon", he wrote.

The need for reform is undoubtedly very clear. The established liberal order was accountable for enforcing austerity measures and strict Eurozone fiscal policies. Brussels as with national governments has to contend with the new force of social media, which acts as a powerful channel to express and magnify the voice of voters discontented and marginalized in society. Facebook, and to a lesser extent Twitter and YouTube, has proven powerful weapons in the Brexit and US presidential 2016 campaigns—successfully winning over potentially millions of voters sidelined by the governing class. The ruling elites in Brussels are acutely aware of voters' demands—but they face the challenge of meeting what in some cases are unrealistic expectations. Globalization has created winners and losers, and European politicians are the first to admit not enough has been done to alleviate the economic disasters of the 2008 global financial crash, and severe and deleterious austerity policies associated with the drastic bailout measures for many Eurozone member states. But, contrary to voter perceptions, the

EU is not a "super-state" but remains a club of nation states pooling their sovereignty through a set of mutual treaties (culminating in the Lisbon Treaty of 2009).[1]

This book will tell the story of what the European Union must become if it is to succeed. It examines how the EU is trying desperately to redefine its pan-European ideals in a bitter fight to re-establish core values—values increasingly undermined by a self-serving (new) breed of "populist" politicians, primarily but not exclusively on the right. Undoubtedly, there has been a lack of transparency in the EU's workings, coupled with a total failure to market its substantial achievements in economic prosperity and social reform. Brussels is perceived as anti-democratic, as pandering to big business and as utterly unsympathetic to the concepts of state borders, national sovereignty and even self-determined democracy. Its policies have fostered regionalism at the expense of the nation state, and resurgent nationalism is an unsurprising result of this.

Historical Context

To understand what the European Union *is*, it needs to be set in its proper, post-war historical context. It is and was originally conceived, as a peace process to unite Europe after the horrors of the Second World War, combined with a customs union and free trade zone, with the Euro bolted on. If we strip away the rhetoric of both advocates and sceptics of the EU, this is what it boils down to in purpose and function.

For 70 years now, the EU has framed the backdrop for relative peace and stability in Europe—from the ashes of the Second World War and all through the Cold War and its turbulent aftermath on the continent (most notably in the breakup of former Yugoslavia). But is this now an end of an era for an inclusive, pan-European order? My answer is simple: no. Populist movements satiate the pressing call for change, but they have no realistic idea of how to effect it. The danger needs to be recognized in its severity. The EU's survival is **not** certain. But there are answers

[1] http://www.europarl.europa.eu/factsheets/en/sheet/5/the-treaty-of-lisbon.

to its challenges—some moderate and some radical—that can, and will, guarantee its future. This book will explain exactly what they are.

It is not just the ongoing Brexit chaos and austerity-related EU disillusionment that are the problems to face up to, but a wider pattern of *identity politics* which is taking place all over Europe, as all the EU's big states (and some small ones) are facing similar upheaval. The latest example of this is Spain, with the resurgence of a right-wing populist party Vox evoking the mantra "Spain first", and even going so far as to celebrate the legacy of Spanish Fascist dictator Franco.[2]

Heading off the threats to the EU's survival includes countering nativist and protectionist forces, both of which represent the breaking of the norms and shared values crafted from the founding treaties. Criticism of EU institutions and the "democratic deficit and lack of transparency" are entirely valid, but exploited for nationalist, nativist and identitarian ends. There has been constant "voter apathy" and low turnout in European Parliamentary elections, and an increased presence from populist parties and forces increasingly threatens the stability of the established party structures. Lack of transparency around the operations of the EU, coupled with a failure to trumpet and market its successes to electorates, only exacerbates this problem and the opportunity for groups seeking to undermine it to thrive.

To forget the original vision of the European Union would amount to a serious blunder for the nation states of Europe, as well as continental Europe as a whole. This includes the UK and Ireland and beyond to the world at large where many countries, through their linkage with the old colonial powers, sacrificed their manpower on the battlefields of mainland Europe in the struggle against Nazism.

Some post-Second World War visionaries could claim the European Union was self-consciously created as an attempt to revive the Roman and Holy Roman Empire—or at least their more redeeming features—namely through a politically united European sphere: one at peace with itself, after two destructive world wars, and one made prosperous by the free flow of goods, people and culture across its borders. Progressing this vision has taken a serious blow in the wake of the populist and nationalist revolts since

[2] *Vox (Latin for "voice") founded by former members of the Peoples' Party (PP).*

the financial and migrant crises, exposing the fragility in the European project faced by the post-2004 and 2007 (ambitious) enlargement.

There was a determined goal by the post-Second World War leaders to put an end to Europe's devastating military conflicts in the nineteenth century's two world wars. This aim more than anything galvanized the founding fathers and statesmen of France, Germany and Italy. It was the collective vision of men like Robert Schuman (France),[3] Konrad Adenauer (Republic of West Germany) and Alcide De Gasperi (Italy) in joining forces with their counterparts in Belgium, the Netherlands and Luxembourg to pioneer the formation of the European Economic Community in 1958. Winston Churchill—reflecting on the need for post-war cooperation—had even expressed the term "United States of Europe" that he used in a famous speech in Switzerland at Zurich University (19 September 1946).

But this was not a call for European *federalism*. Rather, it represented a much more restrained approach and set the tone of UK–EU relations for decades to come. Moreover, Churchill's vision reflected the "Unionist position", i.e. a consultative body, rather than an interstate superstructure. This was contrasted with the vision of politicians on mainland war-torn Europe advancing "the federalist position"—and what has since meant full integration with a {European} constitution.

By the 1950s and 1960s, Europe saw the emergence of two different projects: the European Free Trade Association (EFTA) and the much more political organization of the European Economic Community. Real progress only started in 1951 when the six founding members signed—based on a plan by the French politician Jean Monnet—the European Coal and Steel Community (ECSC). The six European states: France, the Federal Republic of West Germany, Italy and the "Benelux" countries; Belgium, the Netherlands and Luxembourg then signed the Treaty of Rome in 1958. The UK was invited to join but declined, a decision that had a

[3] *Europe day on 9th May marked the anniversary of the 1950 Schuman Declaration when European governments concluded that pooling coal and steel production would make war between historic rivals "not merely unthinkable but materially impossible".*

significant impact on its negotiating position when it finally joined the European Economic Community in 1973 (with Ireland).[4]

The "founding fathers" knew they could end war in Europe by neutralizing the means for making war possible. They stated: "The mission of the ECSC was to contribute to economic expansion, the development of employment and the improvement of the standard of living in the participating countries through the institution" (Treaty of Paris 1951 Article 2, emphasis added). Put simply the aim was to neutralize the means of creating steel production for military aims.

The ECSC integrated the coal and steel industries of Western Europe and was later expanded to include all members of the European Economic Community renamed the European Community and finally the European Union. Although the original treaty was dissolved in 2002, its importance lies in a deliberate effort to avoid wars between France and Germany. Coal and Steel were the means for making the weapons of war, and the ECSC made this impossible. These (visionaries) saw this as merely a first yet important step in progressing European integration. But the ultimate objective was to create a "United States of Europe".

Britain always saw its security interests closely linked to mainland Europe[5] but in other respects has never been "at the heart" of Europe. Historically, it pulled towards the safety of its Commonwealth links, as part of the legacy of Empire, which had come to its rescue in both the First and Second World Wars. From early on, it was the protectionist nature of the Common Agricultural Policy (CAP)[6] and the perceived "supranational" element of the founding Rome Treaty which focused opposition in UK governing elites. Hostility to "closer integration" is shared by many of the new post-2004 accession states challenging this approach, and the following chapters will expand this narrative citing further examples of hostility to "closer union" even among founder members.

---

[4]Britain joined the EEC the forerunner of the EU in January 1973 with Denmark and Ireland, and in a referendum in 1975, the UK electorate voted "yes" by 67.2–32.8% to stay in the EEC under renegotiated terms of entry.

[5]The UK became a founding member of the North Atlantic Treaty Organization (NATO) in 1949.

[6]The CAP is the agricultural policy of the European Union introduced in 1962 providing agricultural subsidies—originally weighted in favour of France and German farmers—costing 71% of the EU budget in 1984. Its proportion of the EU budget has fallen to 39% in 2013. But Eurostat figures show that agriculture still represents less than 2% of EU GDP.

Founding Aims

The current problems facing the EU have to be seen in this historical context and by citing the texts of the Treaty of Rome with the founding fathers: "*AFFIRMING as the essential objective of their efforts the constant improvement of the living and working conditions of their [member states'] peoples" (Preamble to Treaty of Rome 1958).*

European citizens—unless their school curriculum provides for it—may not be aware of the original founding aims of the European Economic Community (EEC), forerunner of the EU in the earlier treaties. But the expansion of those aims, made in a post-war setting, does not invalidate its original purpose. If the original goal was valid for its time, but is now dated, we must consider what ought to be the goal of the EU today. There is an argument/view that the vision of the EU political elites is not in harmony with the aspirations nor the priorities of its EU citizens.

But a political union cannot exist without a firm basis of fundamental political principles. For the sake of a functioning and integrated European Union, its supporting institutions must take the gloves off, so to speak and defend European "values". There will be a long-awaited battle for the soul of Europe. With Brexit, this battle has arguably now begun.

Objectives of the EU

The EU's modern agenda is set out in the Lisbon Treaty Act on 2009, which builds on the legal foundation laid out in earlier major European treaties such as Maastricht Treaty of 1992. Its core principles include, among others:

- the promotion of peace and the well-being of the Union's citizens,
- an area of freedom, security and justice without internal frontiers,
- sustainable development based on balanced economic growth and social justice,
- a social market economy—highly competitive and aiming at full employment and social progress and
- a free single market.

Putting the EU in a historical context and establishing its original aims may enable us to measure its relative success, but most citizens would now argue that it has not achieved at least some of these goals.

The first and most important EU objective was the establishment of a common market. Subsequent treaties included the aims of establishing: an Economic and Monetary Union; a Common Foreign and Security Policy; and an area of Justice and Home Affairs. The Lisbon Treaty includes an even wider range of broad objectives, such as a commitment to "justice", sustainable development and a social market, as noted above.

Recent and current crises have drowned out many of the EU's success stories contributing to the well-being of its citizens. The Union is founded on "respect for human dignity, freedom, democracy, equality, the rule of law and human rights".[7] There have been important regulatory achievements towards these goals, including legislation on consumer rights and employment protection. The EU has been at the forefront in progressing employee rights on discrimination in the workplace and promoting social justice and protection, equality between women and men, solidarity between generations and the protection of children's' rights—all guaranteed by the European Court of Justice (ECJ). These can rightly be claimed by Brussels elites as genuinely being in the interests of their electorates. But ranking higher in priority for most EU citizens is creating jobs, economic growth and investment—including actions to stimulate investment in which less success has been perceived and where expectations have not been met—and where the Europe crisis has generated enormous disappointment and resentment in this regard.

On the plus side, vast budgets have been allocated by Brussels for regional aid through Cohesion and Structural Funds. Both the European Regional Development Fund (ERDF) and the European Social Fund (ESF) have dispensed billions of Euros to regenerate the infrastructures of poor regions to close the gap between the richer and poorer member states. In recent years, the largest beneficiaries of these funds have been Hungary and Poland (and other post-2004 EU beneficiaries states), the

[7] Article 2 TEU 2009.

very members who today defy and ignore the very EU fundamental principles—to which on accession they have subscribed/signed up to—on the rule of law and judicial independence.[8]

The first and most important economic objective was achieved in the establishment of a *common market*. This developed into a thriving *customs union* and *single market* (essentially for goods). The EU 28—soon to be EU27—represents a powerful economic bloc of 500 million consumers with unrivalled commercial power to negotiate free trade agreements (FTAs) with China, Japan and the USA. Individual EU member states would clearly not have the same power and influence to negotiate bilaterally such advantageous commercial terms.

There has been an apparent lack of transparency in its workings, coupled with a total failure to market its achievements. Brussels is perceived as anti-democratic, as pandering to big business and as utterly unsympathetic to the concepts of state borders, national sovereignty and even self-determined democracy.[9] Its policies have fostered regionalism at the expense of the nation state. This makes the current nationalist revival across Europe unsurprising—even as it has been poorly handled by Brussels.

The Long-Awaited Battle for the Soul of Europe

The EU is at a crossroads, and the catalyst for its survival—at least in its present form—may well be decided in the next 5-year parliamentary session. The recent *direct* elections that took place on 25 May 2019, while showing a higher voter turnout (51%), have surprisingly not given the desired outcome for the populist and Eurosceptic parties that they hoped for. Although they did increase their representation, they only won 29% of the seats but this is still their best performance yet—helped by the 29 seats of the UK Brexit Party. The centre-right European People's Party (EPP) remained the largest group, but with a loss of 38 seats and the Socialists

[8]To be discussed in Chapter 6 "Europe's Illiberal democracies".

[9]Allegations that featured prominently in the 2016 UK Brexit campaign.

and Democratic group down 35 seats. Losing their overall majority puts the EU integration agenda on hold without new allies.[10]

Proceedings to start formal meetings of the new session in Strasbourg faced the new MEP intake with hostile speeches from Brexit party MEPs. However, their attendance with other UK MEPs will be cut short if Brexit as scheduled takes place on 31 October 2019, "deal or no deal".[11]

The effect of the UK's exit will be to reduce the total number of MEPs from 751 to 705 seats. With the departure of 73 British MEPs, 27 seats will be re-allocated to member states to better reflect the principle of "degressive proportionality".[12] The 27 seats will be distributed to France (+5), Spain (+5), Italy (+3), the Netherlands (+3), Ireland (+2), Sweden (+1), Austria (+1), Denmark (+1), Finland (+1), Slovakia (+1), Croatia (+1), Estonia (+1), Poland (+1) and Romania (+1), and no member state will lose any seats.[13]

This arrangement is clarified in a proposal by the European Parliament made in February 2018 when the European Council adopted in June of that year a decision on the composition of the European Parliament. This set out the number of representatives in each member state to be elected to the European Parliament for 2019–2024, 9th legislative parliamentary term.[14] The proposal guarantees that seats are dispersed in an "*objective, fair, durable and transparent way* in line with the Treaty on the European Union". The new distribution of seats respects the principle of "degressive proportionality". The latter ensures that larger member states like France and Germany have less seats than smaller states in *proportion* to their population; MEPs from larger member states represent more citizens than those from smaller ones.[15]

[10]The Liberals (the centrist ALDE group) and the Greens (The European Free Alliance) could—with support for their agenda—be potential allies having gained the largest increase in support.

[11]Under the terms agreed with EU leaders in Brussels, the UK was given a Brexit extension until 31 October 2019.

[12]http://www.europarl.europa.eu/RegData/etudes/IDAN/2017/583117/IPOL_IDA%282017%29583117_EN.pdf cf.page 9 of the report.

[13]http://www.europarl.europa.eu/news/en/faq/12/how-many-meps.

[14]EUROPEAN COUNCIL DECISION (EU) 2018/ 937 - of 28 June 2018 …

[15]http://www.europarl.europa.eu/news/en/faq/12/how-many-meps.

The New EU Parliamentary Session

The EU Parliament (EP) opened its new five—year session in Strasbourg on July 2. There were protests in support of Catalan separatists MEPs. They were barred from joining proceedings having failed to pledge their allegiance *in person* to the Spanish constitution. But this incident and the actions of UK Brexit MEPs—snubbing the EU anthem—failed to interrupt parliamentary business.

Proceedings commenced with appointments of presidential candidates and other high-level EU officials. MEPs throughout the member states had fought their election campaigns raising aspirations on effecting change. The parliamentarian's right to scrutinize and approve presidential candidates (and other top officials) was vital to this process. Voters looked to those (candidates) more closely aligned to their political standpoints many of which appear in the text of new Strategic Agenda.

A YouGov poll, conducted in 14 EU member states—representing up to 80% of seats in the European Parliament—canvassed views on a wide range of issues has helped to identify EU citizen's concerns. These covered security issues, migration, climate change, living standards and the economy.[16] The findings of the European Council on Foreign Relations (ECFR), a think tank with its head office based in Berlin[17] showed that European electorates were more concerned with *emigration* and "domestic issues, such as corruption, the cost of living, health, housing, and unemployment".[18]

'A new strategic agenda 2019–2024'[19] set out the four priority areas protecting citizens and freedoms which focused on the following:

- protecting citizens and freedoms,
- developing a strong and vibrant economic base,
- building a climate-neutral, green, fair and social Europe,

---

16 https://www.ecfr.eu/article/european_voters_do_not_consider_migration_most_important_election.

17 Offices in London Madrid, Paris Warsaw Rome and Sofia.

18 Emigration and declining birth rates is discussed in Chapter 5.

19 https://www.consilium.europa.eu/media/39914/a-new-strategic-agenda-2019-2024.pdf.

- promoting European interests and values on the global stage
- and setting out how to achieve those objectives.[20]

In adopting the Strategic Agenda (20 June 2019), the European Council drew attention to effective control of external borders—to allow it to fight illegal migration, agree an effective asylum policy and ensure the proper functioning of Schengen.

The document's text embraced a wide range of challenges, while leaving implementation on detail to the respective EU institutions. Security issues were given critical importance, demonstrating the need to improve collaboration on information-sharing to fight terrorism and cross-border crime and the protection of the EU sphere from malicious cyber activities, hybrid threats and disinformation across all present EU 28, including the UK (after it leaves).[21] Built into MEPs' manifestos, the issues address well-published voters' concerns of citizens. The EU is now charged with realizing/delivering on their expectations.

Europe's **competitiveness, prosperity, jobs and role on the global stage all depend on a strong economic base**. In this field, the European Council is focusing on:

- deepening the Economic and Monetary Union,
- completing the banking and capital markets union,
- strengthening the international role of the euro,
- strengthening cohesion in the EU,
- working on all aspects of the digital revolution and artificial intelligence: infrastructure, connectivity, services, data, regulation and investment,
- reducing the fragmentation of European research, development and innovation activities and
- ensuring fair competition within the EU and on the global stage.[22]

---

[20] https://www.consilium.europa.eu/en/eu-strategic-agenda-2019-2024/.

[21] The EU's co-operation with a post-Brexit Britain would be a vital component of this policy.

[22] https://www.consilium.europa.eu/en/eu-strategic-agenda-2019-2024/.

But new political re-alignments will now have to take stock of the increased representation of the Greens and the Liberals championing their (ambitious) agendas on climate change and the environment. Right-wing and Eurosceptic MEPs are not yet in alliance, and the parties remain fragmented. In the short term, Parliament will be a more unpredictable body, as parties form groupings and determine their policy positions. Simon Kuper, writing in the Financial Times on 23 March 2019, remarked that the challenge for the EU in the next few years is not "*Leave Euroscepticism*"—namely the British form that manifested with full force in the Brexit vote—but "*Remain Euroscepticism*", a label that can be aligned with Hungary's Prime Minister Viktor Orban—a leading beneficiary of EU funds. Kuper suggests the ultimate challenge will come from "Eurosceptic Remainers"—those powerful Eurosceptic opinions that seek to reform the EU from *within* but with no desire to leave the EU. There are others like Matteo Salvini, the leader of the Lega (Nord) party in Italy, and Jean-Luc Mélénchon in France who echo this approach.[23]

Actions to Revive the European Project

The May elections stand to be a reality check on Brussels' past record in achieving priorities set out by (EU) Commission President Jean-Claude Junker for his tenure and Commission mandate for the period 2015–2019. These have been summarized as:

1. Jobs, growth and investment: Stimulating investment and creating jobs,
2. Digital single market: Bringing down barriers to unlock online opportunities,
3. Energy union and climate: Making energy more secure, affordable and sustainable,
4. Internal market: A deeper and fairer internal market,
5. A deeper and fairer Economic and Monetary Union: Combining stability with fairness and democratic accountability,

[23] https://www.ft.com/simon-kuper, 23/24 March 2019.

6. A balanced and progressive trade policy to harness globalization: Open trade—without sacrificing Europe's standards,
7. Justice and fundamental rights: Enhancing cooperation between different EU justice systems and preserving the rule of law,
8. Migration: Towards a European agenda on migration,
9. A stronger global actor: Strengthening the global role of Europe and
10. Democratic change: Making the EU more transparent and democratically accountable.

While the EU remains a bastion for promoting justice, social change and democratic values, Jean-Claude Junker's legacy may not be so kind in evaluating what has to be the main priority of his mandate for "Jobs, growth and investment: Stimulating investment and creating jobs". But progress has been made. In the first quarter of 2018, the ratio of vacancies to total jobs reached its highest level since Eurostat data became available in 2008. In addition, the EU's overall unemployment rate fell to 7.1% in April 2018[24]—the same level as in September 2007, just before the global financial crisis.[25]

Progress has been made in bringing down barriers to unlock online opportunities, aiming for an inclusive digital society which benefits from the single market. The EU agenda on Migration[26] vital to defusing tensions with anti-immigration populist parties has made sustained progress. EU actions have been taken in control of the central and western Mediterranean routes, reinforcing arrangements with Turkey on the Aegean entry points to be discussed in Chapter 4. A progressive trade policy to date has led to the signing of thirty-six FTAs with non-EU countries the most recent being the EU-Singapore Free Trade Agreement (EUSFTA). The EU-Japan deal ratified on 8 December 2018 created a trading zone of 635 million people representing a third of global GDP.

---

[24] *The unemployment in Spain stood at 14.7% in first quarter of 2009 and with the seasonally adjusted rate in Greece down to 18.5% in February 2019.*

[25] https://www.ft.com/content/718c3892-73c5-11e8-aa31-31da4279a601.

[26] https://ec.europa.eu/policies/european....

The New EU Parliament—Populism

Even with strategic alliances between them, populists' parties have yet to formulate a common reforming agenda and won't necessarily be able to control the legislation programme in the new session, as their parliamentary representation doesn't allow for it. All the EU Parliamentary elections have shown a greater degree of fragmentation threatening established party coalitions. It is very clear, therefore, that the new EU Parliament will have to bolster its strength and resilience to nativist and populist forces. A recent analysis suggests their rise may have reached a "high-water mark", but this remains to be seen.[27] The newly appointed EU Commission President, Ursula von der Leyen, officially in post from November 1 will need to develop a menu of actions to avert political disruption from the Eurosceptic and populist groups—a monumental challenge that can only be met by seriously addressing the main priorities of the Strategic Agenda as discussed. Her appointment by the European Council had bypassed the "spitzenkandidaten process".[28] But Jill Evans MEP (Plaid Cymru) has noted.... that as part of her manifesto, Ursula von der Leyen has promised that she will support a two year conference starting in 2020 on the "Future of the EU" and she is committed to involving citizens as much as possible in having an input into that... "She is also open to the idea of a member of the European Parliament chairing this Conference and has committed to bringing forward a European Green Deal in her first 100 days as President".[29]

The EU Parliament can rightly claim its democratic credentials vis-à-vis other EU institutions. It is elected directly by EU citizens through a proportional representation method of voting. The Maastricht Treaty (1992) empowered it to approve (and, therefore, also to reject) the Commission as a body before it took office. The treaty also requires that Parliament to be consulted by member states before they nominated the person to be appointed as EU Commission President. Currently, the candidate for the President of the Commission is proposed by the European Council,

---

[27] https://www.bloomberg.com/graphics/2019-european-parliament-populism/.

[28] A German term for lead candidate referring to a European political party's lead candidate for EU Commission President.

[29] Interview with Jill Evans MEP 5/9/2019.

but the latter must do so while "taking into account" the parliamentary elections and "after having held the appropriate consultations" (Article 17(7) TEU). The President is elected by the Parliament by a majority of its component members (376 of 751 votes or 353 of 705 post-Brexit).[30] The centre-right European Peoples' Party (EPP) and centre-left Socialists and Democrats (S&D), following the recent EU elections, have lost their dominance, and without forming alliances with other groups, the tilt of their agenda on measures towards further integration remains unlikely.

Some analysts are focusing on the continued rise of right-wing anti-establishment movements and the growing tensions between Brussels and post-2004 accession members over adherence to EU values and the rule of law, while others express the need for the EU to expand its responsibilities in matters such as security, terrorism, migration[31] and taxation where it has already made a good start.[32] Globally, other governments also face radical and reactionary forces united in opposing social-liberal democracies perceived as defenders of global capitalism and big business and corrupt regimes.[33]

At an event in Gothenburg Sweden on 17 November 2017, the presidents of the European Commission and Parliament, Jean-Claude Juncker and Antonio Tajani, with Estonian Prime Minister Juri Ratas signed a so-called "European Pillar of Social Rights" promising to "put the best interest of our citizens in the heart of the EU agenda".[34]

This statement, based on the document, accepted the need for concerted action to stem the potential fallout from the 2016 UK Brexit vote. It triggered a series of efforts to tackle rising populism in the European Union, focusing on strengthening the social aspect of the EU's role in protecting workers and assisting the disadvantaged.

Twenty principles were adopted, ranging from gender equality to fair wages to assisting the homeless. Social policies vary widely across Europe, so implementation will be in the hands of member states. "If we allow

---

[30]Ten issues to watch in 2019—europarl.europa.eu. http://www.europarl.europa.eu/RegData/etudes/IDAN/2019/630352/EPRS_IDA(2019)630352_EN.pdf.

[31]Migration Chapter 4.

[32]European Parliamentary briefing 22 March 2019.

[33]Election of Jair Bolsonaro a populist right-wing Brazilian politician 1 January 2019.

[34]https://ec.europa.eu/priorities/europea….

unemployment to grow due to unfair practices, if jobs are left vacant because young people lack proper education or parents haven't received retraining, then social discord in our countries will grow", the host, Swedish Prime Minister Stefan Loefven said.

"After challenges and uncertainty in the EU in recent years, I firmly believe that the best way to increase trust in the EU and in its institutions is that to bring about real improvement in people's daily lives", he added in a joint press conference with Jean-Claude Juncker (EU Commission President) and European Council President Donald Tusk.[35] "Today we have shown this does not need to be the case… Today has shown, there is a clear commitment to put the best interest of our citizens in the heart of the EU agenda", Loefven, a Social Democrat representative, added.

It was clear that even before the May elections, EU citizens had to put aside their usual (voter) apathy if they wished to reinforce the European project under attack from nativist anti-elitist forces on the left and right of European politics. The message was successful to the extent that it showed increased voter turnout to 51%, a point raised by Jill Evans MEP stating that: "*which was not expected and should give Parliament more leverage*",[36] with the Greens and Liberals gaining most, although populists saw some increases too.[37] Matteo Salvini, Italy's deputy prime minister and leader of its far-right League party, continues to work to form a grand alliance of European right-wing parties for the European Parliamentary elections. This could include Austria's ruling coalition of the conservative Austrian People's Party, and the radical-right Freedom Party may also join an alliance. While Le Penn's French National Rally party may join, it is not yet certain whether Hungary's Fidesz party will be an ally in Salvini's coalition—although its leader Viktor Orban has expressed solidarity with Salvini. Fidesz is still technically a member of the European People's Party (EPP). But it has recently been suspended from the EPP for its anti-Brussels rhetoric and breaches of the rule of law contrary to EU rules.

[35] https://euobserver.com/social/139922.

[36] Recognition of the democratic legitimacy of the EU Parliament although no right in the treaties to initiate legislation.

[37] https://www.bbc.co.uk/news/live/world-europe-48389690.

How the New European Parliament Will Be Different

The 2019 European elections are the first when a member state (the UK) is in the process of leaving the EU club. The departure date and process still remain unclear as the UK Parliament has not signed off the EU–UK Withdrawal Agreement. As a result, after decades of growth in EU parliamentary membership, the Parliament will become smaller—the number of members for 2019–2024 will be reduced to 705 from 751. The number of members will remain unchanged until UK's departure actually takes place.

With the UK's involvement, EU policymaking could suffer havoc with long-term EU–UK relations. On these issues, the outstanding guide is "The European Elections and Brexit", a report by the UK in a Changing Europe, a research group at King's College London.[38] In the UK, the birth of the "Brexit" party is of much more concern to both Conservatives and Labour politicians as it is ahead in the polls with 35% of the vote albeit a protest vote with no political manifesto except to leave the EU if necessary with "no deal".

The EU Parliamentary elections seem certain to produce a more fragmented European Parliament. The two main party groups on the centre-right and centre-left are set to lose their combined majority. A hotchpotch of right-wing nationalists, anti-establishment populists and anti-EU critics may win 30% or so of the assembly's 751 seats.

Such an outcome could destabilize the EU Parliament's cross-party consensus on Brexit held since the UK's June 2016 referendum. It may also result in the appointment of a European Commission that would reconsider the Brexit line of Jean-Claude Juncker, outgoing Commission President, and Michel Barnier, the EU's chief Brexit negotiator. There is also the prospects of a future EU–UK trade deal, relationship on security, sharing of intelligence on terrorism and migration matters post-Brexit.

[38]https://www.ft.com/content/7d750460-717e-11e9-bf5c-6eeb837566c5.

In fact, ratification of an EU–UK trade agreement might be a Herculean task in a European Parliament pushed one way by right-wing protectionism and another way by left-wing demands on climate change, regulatory standards and social policy.

Is the USA an Existential Threat?

The simple answer is probably *no*—although actions on the ground may appear to suggest otherwise. The Trump administration, personified by Trump himself, demonstrates a deep disdain for dealing with multinational organizations even in his own backyard. This was clearly evidenced by his behaviour with neighbours in the revision of the NAFTA trade treaty with Canada and Mexico accusing both countries of stealing American jobs with an unfair balance of trade. The USA withdrew from the Trans-Pacific Partnership (TTP) and is in a retaliatory trade conflict with China which if pursue could threaten to destabilize global commerce.

This pattern of US protectionism and hostility with doing business through multilateral treaties—preferring bilateral agreements—extends to relations with Europe. Trump has nothing but contempt for EU institutions and for the social and democratic values it champions. Trump has shown to be more at home with autocrats and dictators than working with long-standing democratic alliances.

The European Union is supposedly where the USA has its staunchest political and military allies in NATO. But as with China and Japan is no exception to the imposition of tariffs with Trump singling out the German auto industry. His administration's first act on this front was to impose steel and aluminium tariffs by invoking a "national security" provision and refusing to exempt allies in Europe and Canada.

In tense relations with the EU, Trump has singled out Merkel's Germany in particular for criticism for both failing to raise defence spending (to 2% agreed among NATO member but only by 2024) and for continued EU–UK trade imbalances. On the political front, US diplomats are seen to be courting Europe's populist leaders ahead of the EU Parliamentary elections which could be taken as a deliberate slight on Europe's more established centrist party leaders. For example, in blatant contrast to

President Trump's habit of railing against the leaders of Germany, France, Britain, Canada and other democratic allies, he has deliberately courted Hungary's "illiberal" strongman at a bilateral venue in the Presidential Oval Office on 13 May only 10 days before European elections. In the meeting, Trump referred to Viktor Orban as a highly respected leader who was doing a tremendous job: "You have been great with respect to Christian communities, you have really put a block up [against non-Christian immigration]".[39]

The forces of liberal democracy may appear to be on the defensive, but the EU's real problem is not Trump's America—even if it continues to drive a wedge between Germany (and France) and his new found "populist" friends. Polls still show that post-2004 accession states are still pro-EU. A new survey in 2018 by CBOS showed that 92% of the electorate wanted to remain in the EU.[40] But future economic benefits of membership will be tied to adherence to the rule of law and other fundamental freedoms. Both Poland and Hungary are on notice of sanctions for breaches of EU law. The EU Commission has its crisis management in top gear to deal with the insurgent Italian coalition, but Salvini and his Eurosceptic partners in Central Europe will have difficulty creating the majority (in the EU Parliament) needed to disrupt EU institutions from a pro-European stance. The election of Zuzana Čaputová as President in Slovakia is evidence that parties with a pro-European agenda can still win elections.[41] With Brexit on the horizon, the EU's financial largess directed eastwards since 2004 will be reduced—with the loss of the British contribution. Rich northern states like Germany, the Netherlands and Finland express no appetite to fill the budgetary financial gap.

[39] https://www.newyorker.com/magazine/2018/12/24/how-trump-made-war-on-angela-merkel-and-europe.

[40] https://www.independent.co.uk/news/world/europe/poland-eu-membership-support-for-membership.

[41] See Populism Chapter 5.

External Threats to the EU Project

The European Union may be "dis"-united in many fundamental issues like immigration, the rule of law and the Eurozone, but when it comes to Brexit, the EU27 members closed ranks. Regarding the growth of populism, what is striking is that although the "populist" parties made their advance, they didn't make their political advance as much as they had hoped. They remain well short of their swing vote in the European Parliament. In Greece, it was the centre-right party that won their general election on 7 July 2019 and *not* the anti-European party.

The UK is a net contributor to the EU budget, and members have been united on extracting what is owed to meet British financial obligations. The efforts made by the UK with Theresa May racing around European capitals during negotiations to "*divide et impera*"—a trait used from its colonial past—fell on deaf ears. Money and Citizens Rights were the EU 27's own red lines and that's before any final trade negotiations in the "transitional period". That said Brexit is recognized by all parties to be Europe's biggest turning point.

Both President Macron and Chancellor Merkel have cautioned EU members to remain united against external threats; "there is no doubt that Europe needs to reposition itself in a changing world" Merkel said recently:

> "There is no doubt that Europe needs to reposition itself in a changed world," Merkel said in a conversation in her office in Berlin. "The old certainties of the post-war order no longer apply." Addressing external challenges posed to the EU by its three main global rivals, China, United States and Russia.

These challenges range from Russian interference in elections, territorial ambitions to the EU's east to China's economic power enticing Italy and Greece to join (the European end) its Belt and Road Initiative. These and the US trade threats necessitate the EU to remain united. Merkel adds that: "Simply stating that we've enjoyed seven decades of peace is no longer enough to justify the European project. Without forward-looking arguments to justify Europe, the European peace project would also be in greater jeopardy than one may think".[42]

One of the biggest strategic questions facing the EU and the whole European project is how to position itself in a world dominated by the USA and China, in a superpower rivalry being played out by different rules. Courtesy of Donald Trump, the EU is operating against a background of an incoherent and unpredictable US foreign policy which ignores both America's long-standing allies and the advice of key internal advisers, bodies and institutions. For the EU's part, it must be seen to take a strong stand against Russia on Eastern Ukraine, on Iran where it (at present) holds steadfast to the Joint Comprehensive Plan of Action (JCPOA) Nuclear Treaty. This is in defiance of the USA, who unilaterally exited the Iran nuclear deal on 8 May 2018, consequently re-imposing punitive sanctions on Iran. It is axiomatic that the "Brussels" effect recognized in the context of trade and economic policy must extend and translate into a robust and credible foreign policy which, while working with the USA, holds the latter to account where necessary.

[42] https://www.theguardian.com/.../angela-merkel-interview-europe-eu-unite-challenge-us-....

2

The Survival of the Euro?

Saving the EU's southern flank; Greece and default threat from Italy; Efforts to Confront Weakness in the Eurozone; Economic analysis/assessment of the impact of Brexit on trade, value chains, innovation in the EU27. Is the Euro a bulwark against the dollar? The Euro—a weapon to enhance global power. Its potential role as a reserve currency.

The Survival of the Euro: "Whatever It Takes"

At a speech in London on 26 July 2012, the President of the European Central Bank (ECB) gave a stark account of the state of the Eurozone economy. Bond yields of weak Euro-member governments were soaring, and international markets were questioning whether national governments, Euro or EU-level institutions could act appropriately to prevent economic disaster. Mario Draghi's—the ECB President—task was to calm nervous markets and convince international investors that the Eurozone economy wasn't about to collapse.

J. Theodore, *Survival of the European (Dis) Union*,
https://doi.org/10.1007/978-3-030-31214-5_2

Clearly, the Eurozone was seen by some to be in terminal decline, with numerous bailouts in play to rescue debt-ridden member states—a crisis jeopardizing the very existence of the currency union. But Draghi will always be remembered for his famous phrase: "whatever it takes". His message of reassurance was that: "Within our mandate, the ECB is ready to do whatever it takes to preserve the euro. And believe me, it will be enough".[1]

This may have to be the approach for the next ECB President as well, after Mario Draghi stands down on 31 October 2019. But will there be a willingness to renew the promise to do "*whatever it takes*" to stop the euro failing. A failure to do so may produce an "existential issue for potential crisis countries, especially for those too big for the ESM [European Stability Mechanism]"—Italy in particular. It generally remains "a question for the stability of the monetary union as a whole", whereas "far-reaching deepening of the monetary union" could change the market perception of how safe sovereign bonds are", he said, concluding that "It's a very touchy issue".[2] Angela Merkel has recently indicated her vision of a future European Monetary Fund (EMF) and an investment budget designed to address "structural weaknesses" in euro area countries. But her concept of an EMF remains closely aligned to German financial orthodoxy: in that it is seen as a tool for strengthening budgetary discipline, rather than the new, bigger instrument for fighting future financial crises in the Eurozone as proposed by President Macron.

Merkel said that the IMF should play a role in surveying national public finances and that its long-term loans would be contingent on "wide-ranging structural reforms" and only awarded "when the whole Eurozone is in danger". It would also have "appropriate instruments that could be used when necessary to restore [a Eurozone member's debt sustainability]", in an apparent nod to the possibility of sovereign bond restructuring. Italy would also reject such an idea, said Lucas Guttenberg, a senior research fellow at the Delors Institute in Berlin. "It could change the market perception of how safe sovereign bonds are", he said. "It's a very touchy issue".[3]

[1] https://qz.com/1038954/whatever-it-takes-five-years-ago-today-mario-draghi-saved-the-euro-with-a-momentous-speech/.

[2] https://strengtheningeurope.eu/…/a-missed-opportunity-five-reasons-why-esm-reform-….

[3] https://www.ft.com/content/0b0bd67a-6706-11e8-8cf3-0c230fa67aec.

If keeping the Eurozone intact requires maintaining an absolute commitment to "whatever it takes", there may well be other challenges for which the next ECB President will need to find adequate solutions.

Germany and EMU

It was Chancellor Helmut Kohl who was the driving force in the unification of the Federal Republic of West Germany and East Germany (DDR) on 3 October 1990. This was a colossal achievement requiring international support from USA, UK and the tacit approval of the Soviets and France. There was of course a heavy financial price to pay for the Federal Republic in giving up its 3:1 Deutschmark/Ostmark supremacy, by allowing parity for the Ostmark—a steep financial price for West Germany, but one deemed worth paying for the unification process. The 1:1 exchange rate, apart from ensuring price transparency, also guaranteed the purchasing parity of savings in East Germany thus preventing a run on the banks in the East, which would have to be bailed out by the West anyway.

For Helmut Kohl, the vision of greater (EU) integration would be strengthened by a currency union with Germany as a prime mover (with France) for a broad and comprehensive Economic and Monetary Union. Kohl was noted for creating a narrative "that the euro was an instrument of peace", which many critics have subsequently claimed (with hindsight) was not a good idea.[4] However, it has to be noted that the country that paid the highest price for the creation of the European Monetary Union (EMU) was France. Following German re-unification massive increases in government expenditure took place in the Eastern parts of the country driving inflation close to 10%. This was anathema to the Bundesbank which reacted by increasing interest rates. However, this took place in the background of an international slowdown in growth, warranting a decrease in interest rates. The UK and Italy, not able to withstand the increase in interest rates following German re-unification, left the Exchange Rate Mechanism in August 1992, with Italy re-joining in November 1996. France did not follow through with the UK and Italy and remained in the

[4] M. Feldstein. (1997). "EMU and International Conflict", *Foreign Affairs*, 76, pp. 60–74.

system in order to "honour" the French franc–Deutsche Mark exchange rate parity. As a result, throughout the 1990s, France paid on average in excess of 9% interest in order to finance her debt obligations. The French debt-to-GDP ratio, from one of the lowest in the EU at only 41% in 1991, reached 62% by 1999 (Marsh 2009). The Bundesbank rejected adopting other policies, such as accommodative monetary policy, due to their potential inflationary impact. As a result, in similar fashion to the way the ECB rejected Quantitative Easing Programmes from 2010 to 2015, Germany has exerted immense deflationary pressures to the rest of the EU twice in the last three decades.

For Germany and France, a currency union was a critical element in the process of evolving further European integration. With German politicians, however, this never meant a true fiscal union—with all its implications. In a speech on 24 April 1998 (in the Bundestag), Kohl made it clear that "Germany will not pay the bills of other member states"—a statement which has since set the tone for Germany's approach throughout the last decade of Eurozone crises. Germany was asserting its national interest. This led to a policy of austerity economics imposed on Eurozone debtor nations: one pursued with tenacious precision by Wolgang Schauble, Germany's finance minister, especially against Greece in the brutal bailout packages offered to the ailing nation in 2010–2018.

Pro-integrationist politicians eagerly advanced the economic rationale for EMU. The elimination of separate currencies would provide stable exchange rates and promote economic growth and shared prosperity.[5] In the early years, Eurozone economies enjoyed benefits from lower interest rates. International investors assumed that the discipline of a single currency would force the less rich Euro members to grow their economies and gauged that lending risk would be supported/bailed out by others—ergo, if lending risk declined, then more credit would be subsequently available.[6]

With low interest rates, a credit boom soon followed in Greece, Ireland and Portugal, Italy and Spain (the PIIGS). But the effect of the global

[5]In 1999, the Euro replaced 11 national currencies and today 19.

[6]The euro area today (the region composed of countries in the European Monetary Union or EMU) has nominal gross domestic product (GDP) of roughly $13.8 trillion, making it the second-largest economic bloc in the world after the USA.

financial crash in 2007–2009 put these countries into recession with the decline in global trade. Increasing debt forced reliance on credit from central banks and the IMF and governments reduced public spending and raise taxes. Bailouts imposed tough conditions and decades of austerity, mass unemployment and low growth for these debtor nations, sowing the seed for voter resentment now seen in the populist movements today.

Germany and other (northern) creditor nations from the start benefited from strong exports financed by credit from debtor countries' banks. This inevitably created a North–South divide, geographically and economically, between the richer Northern EU states including Germany, France and the Benelux countries (Belgium, the Netherlands and Luxembourg) and those members on the Mediterranean littoral. The draconian bailout terms for those states provided finance, but also prompted debate about reverting to national currencies—but to abandon the euro at favourable exchange rates would be impossible, as even for Greece to return to the drachma would have led to a catastrophic currency devaluation.

Greece and the Default Threat from Italy

By 2010, the attention of the international financial community was rapidly focused on Greece, the weakest link in a brittle chain of Euro-zone economies. Greece had been living beyond its means even before it joined the euro. The country was only allowed to join the euro by blatant mis-accounting that hid the equivalent of 10 billion euros in its debt. In a now notorious financial manoeuvre, Goldman Sachs helped the country obscure the true extent of its debt—limited by Maastricht Treaty rules to 60% of GDP and a 3% deficit—through a credit swap scheme that engineered an artificially low public deficit within the maximum entry criteria. But after the country joined the single currency, public spending soared. Wages in the public sector rose over 50% between 1999 and 2008. Around 10 billion was consumed by the 2004 Olympic Games in Athens. As money flowed out of government coffers, revenues were increasingly redirected towards debt repayments—a process which accelerated exponentially after the financial crisis and culminated in Greece's near debt-default and bailouts in 2010–2011.

The IMF-EU austerity measures that followed with a series of bailout interventions have effectively seen Greece reduced from an economically "developed" to an underdeveloped nation. Sources from the Greek side close to senior officials in Brussels, who wished to remain anonymous, suggest in strong, somewhat robust language that "the middle class are being pauperized and destroyed" and that, despite an awareness of their own economic mismanagements, they feel "a sense of betrayal by their European partners". They further add that "all the evidence points to the fact that the consequences of the austerity measures on its citizens is to promote social unrest on a worrying scale, and has promoted the growth of extremism as seen in the European election in May 2014".

Such opinions find plenty of corroboration in the data. Underpinning the rationale of these policies has been the notion that Greece—as well as Ireland, Spain and Portugal—can recover by means of an internal pricing devaluation as an alternative to the currency devaluation that a single currency straitjackets away as an option. This has meant increasing unemployment through austerity measures to the point that wages fall enough to make the country more internationally competitive.

But the social costs of such a move are extremely high—and the evidence it works thin. At the time, unemployment doubled in Greece (to 27%), more than doubled in Spain (to 24.7%) and more than tripled in Ireland (to 14.7%). It took years for sustained recovery to materialize. The biggest problem facing a government in an austerity-driven economic spiral is how it can service debt repayments from an ever-dwindling source of revenue instead of investing in infrastructure and economic development (Wyplosz 2014). This was always the main contention of the Greeks throughout the darkest years of austerity. Overall, €336 billion was provided to the country in order to meet debt obligations, in the form of three bailouts from 2010 to 2018, with almost €300 billion used by the Greek authorities. These sums will cover the country's debt obligations up to 2022. Of these, 91% were used to ensure the country does not default, and only the remaining 9% was directed towards investment programmes.[7]

[7]http://theconversation.com/greece-exits-its-third-bailout-but-eurozone-still-has-much-to-learn-from-the-crisis-101709.

Small businesses (SMEs), the main drivers of a modern economy, closed down at the rate of 5000 per month—not to mention the other 100,000 which have gone bankrupt since 2008. Those SME businesses that were actually able to trade and conduct business failed to grow as interest rates on loans are so prohibitively high in Greece, in contrast to what at the time were effectively "negative" interest rates in Germany: a scenario in which German banks in effect paid the debtor to borrow from them. These circumstances are ironic, considering the EU's treasured ambition to enable the private sector to regenerate employment in Europe.[8]

Whether in fact it would have been easier for Greece to exit the single currency—aside from the constitutional crisis in the Eurozone and likely contagion effect—and undergo monetary devaluation is an important question to ask when looking at the calamitous effect of a single currency on the southern states of post-financial crisis Europe. EU ministers warned of a sharp increase in Greek debt from such a sharp currency devaluation (likely over half and up to two-thirds) if it were to have left the Eurozone. The infrastructure of the single currency rendered these options impossible for member states such as Greece. In any event, this possibility is now a historical counter-factual, whose final answer we will never know.

From a creditors' point of view—the views of which European Union authorities had apparently adopted—a country that has accumulated too much debt must be punished, so as not to encourage "bad behaviour" and to prevent moral hazard. A chief Merkel economic advisor went as far as to say that emergency bailouts to Greece and future EU aid recipients should bring with it deliberately harsh and punitive penalties. But punishing an entire country for the past mistakes of its leaders or governing class, while apparently morally satisfying to some, was hardly the basis for sound and sustainable policy. Indeed, it is worth noting in this respect the special irony that France and Germany were among the first countries to break the Stability and Growth Pact—an agreement which forbids member states to have more than 3% of budget deficit to GDP, while Spain and Ireland ran surpluses before the 2008 crisis. Germany was in breach of the deficit/debt rule in 1998–1999, 2002–2005 and 2008–2010. Such a fact sits ill at ease

[8] Dr. D. Syrrakos an expert on Eurozone economics is a member of Future Economies University Research Centre at Manchester Metropolitan University interviewed on 16 and 23 June 2019.

with the unyielding rhetoric from the France and Germany about the indulgent and dissolute behaviour of the profligate South.

Default Threat from Italy

Arguably, Italy's budget crisis remains a bigger threat to the EU than Brexit. This is because Italy—the third biggest economy in the Eurozone has the capacity to destroy the European single currency, the Euro. While Britain is a major budgetary contributor, its planned forthcoming exit will impact EU finances overall, but not in direct respect of the Euro, as it is not in the Eurozone, unlike Italy. The latter country's public finances, like its banking system, are long-standing problems and constantly under scrutiny (by international markets) and the European Commission. Italy's debt-to-GDP ratio stands at 135% and is the second highest in the EU after Greece—its sovereign debt level, at €2.37 trillion, by far the highest.[9]

Brussels has warned Italy's populist government by letter over its rising debt levels, setting up a fresh clash between the EU and Rome less than a week after European elections. The European Commission on Wednesday wrote to Italy's finance ministry asking for an explanation on the country's deteriorating debt situation. "Italy is confirmed not to have made sufficient progress towards compliance with the debt criterion for 2018", said a letter cosigned by Valdis Dombrovskis, Vice-President for the Eurozone, and Pierre Moscovici, Commissioner for the economy.[10] The letter acts as Stage 1 in a process made by the EU Commission's to evaluate the deterioration in Italy's public debt and budget deficit. This is not an uncommon procedure but puts Italy's new government on notice that it must be in compliance with mandated budget debt limits of 60% of GDP. Stage 1 letters have also been sent to Belgium and Cyprus.

Previously, the European Commission had already warned the new government against increasing the budget deficit and its national debt threatening sanctions/fines for violating budget discipline. Tensions with the EU Commission were initially resolved with an agreement to keep to

[9]https://www.bloomberg.com/articles/t....

[10]https://www.ft.com/content/83462010-821b-11e9-9935-ad75bb96c849?desktop=true&segmentId=d8d3e364-5197-20eb-17cf-2437841d178a#myft:notification:instant-email:content.

a forecasted deficit of 2.04% of GDP for 2019—but this is seen as only a temporary solution to the overall problem of Italy's finances.

The Italian banks are heavily saddled with government debt that could lead to a default similar to the Greek banking crisis in 2012 crisis. The (Italian) government relies on the banks to lend it enough money to carry on. "The Italian banks and treasury are like two drunken giants propping each other up, inextricably linked by mutual weakness. When the crisis hits, they will go down together".[11] With the departure of Mario Draghi (in October 2019), there is no guarantee that Italy will have influence on the ECB board. The new populist leader Matteo Salvini, leader of the right-wing League, said earlier that the leadership of the Bank of Italy should be "zeroed" for failing to protect savers during the country's banking crisis.[12] His coalition partner, Luigi Di Maio, leader of the broadly anti-establishment Five Star Movement, turned his criticism on Draghi's decision to halt the ECB's €2.6 trillion Quantitative Easing (QE). This programme is unsustainable without a wider reform of the Eurozone and integration into a fiscal union, a policy that President Macron proposes but which is not supported by Chancellor Merkel.

Regarding future representation by Italy on the board of the ECB, this would be expected for political reasons: "Italy should have a seat no matter what other country the future ECB president comes from", said Melvyn Krauss, a senior fellow at Stanford University's Hoover Institution. "Italy is a country with great central banking talent … when Axel Weber dropped out eight years ago and Berlin, much like this time, could not find a suitable German candidate, the Italians actually had two - Mario Draghi and Lorenzo Bini-Smaghi".[13]

The pressure on the Italian coalition will now be to make good on their election promises. Their hostility to the EU is not to leave, but to change it from within, by pursuing a populist agenda of anti-immigration and devolving more powers back to national control. There will be pressure from voters now expecting anti-austerity measures which would lead to borrow and spend policies which Italy can ill afford.

[11] https://www.independent.co.uk/voices/italy-budget-crisis-brexit-eu-economics-public-services-giuseppe-conte-matteo-salvini-a8597466.html.

[12] https://finanz.dk/italy-faces-loss-of-ecb-influence-when-mario-draghi-leaves/.

[13] https://www.ft.com.

Although Italians have no desire to leave the EU or even the Eurozone, they have become "Euro-hostile" rather than "Eurosceptic" and determined that it should work in their interests—connotations of the Trump election campaign mantra except, in this case, branded "Italy First". Sooner or later, it is likely this approach will provoke another Eurozone crisis. The flaws in the single currency are real and have not gone away since the Greek financial debacle and other Eurozone crises. In each case, financial rescue demanded members to deflate when they became uncompetitive without the ability to devalue their currency (boxed in as they are by a fixed exchange rate). Deflationary policies have meant cutting public services and wages, as in Greece, which led to a sharp decline in popularity of the governing Italian centrist parties of both left and right.

Greece's economy may at the time have been small enough to save via a bailout programme. But Italy's is *not*: and for that reason, it must not fail. The survival of the Euro depends on this not happening. If Germany wasn't enthusiastic about bailing out Greece, even with the most punitive economic terms, then it certainly won't bail out Italy. In any event, a financial rescue of Italy would be beyond Germany's financial (and political) ability to implement. As the third largest economy in the Eurozone, and with its sovereign/national debt at 2.37 trillion euros, investors would fear an Italian default precipitating the disintegration of the Eurozone, its banking sector and political instability spreading economic contagion throughout Europe.

With the arrival of the populist coalition, the crisis in Italy has broadened beyond simply economics into a much larger political standoff. A policy of undermining the unity of the European Union has been threefold: blocking the EU's recognition (supported by the USA) of the supporters of the coup in Venezuela as the legitimate "elected" authority; opposing the implementation of further EU led sanctions against Russia; and offering support for the "gilets jeunes" or "yellow vest" movement in France, much to the annoyance of the Macron government. More importantly, Italy is once more slipping into recession with negative economic growth. Italian banks face deep financial problems burdened with over 185 billion euros of non-performing loans (NPLs) higher than in any other EU state—although Greece has a higher percentage (45%) of NPLs by comparison.[14] The Italian economic crisis could have serious consequences for the entire European banking system.

On the one hand, the EU Commission could (inadvertently) push Italy to the brink of bankruptcy—or even trigger economic crisis and a likely implosion of the current government. If this happened, there is a very real risk that Italy could declare either a default on its government debt, and/or even an exit from the Eurozone. Ironically, the institutions worst hit by such a scenario will be French banks, which Bloomberg[15] estimates have Italian loans worth hundreds of billions of euros on their balance sheets. Such a shock would very likely see foreign investors—even *European* ones—diverting their holdings and leaving the Eurozone, adding a currency component to the banking crisis. Time will tell whether the European Commission proves willing to take those risks to punish Italy's government, but we can already agree with Luigi Di Maio, Italy's deputy prime minister, who, after meeting the French "yellow vests", stated (on Twitter) that "the winds of change have crossed the Alps".[16] Populist politicians in Europe love comparing the European Union to the late USSR, with its failing, highly centralized federal structure, and this comparison is starting to ring true like it never has before.

Efforts to Confront Weakness in the Eurozone

The Italian economy's return to recession in February 2019 implies that the Italian authorities are presented yet again with renewed pressure from the Italian public, the EU Commission and debt investors. While in 2017 bond investors increased their holdings of Italian debt by €13 billion, in 2018 they reduced their holdings by €60 billion. This places additional pressure on the Italian government when seeking to finance the country's debt, considering that authorities have to service a staggering €250 billion

[14] www.economist.com.

[15] The contagion factor of non-Italian banks' credit exposure to Italy, as of June 2018: France 285B, Germany 58.78B, Belgium 25.2B, Spain 21.4B and the UK 17.4B.

[16] https://www.reuters.com/article/us-france-italy/italys-di-maio-meets-french-yellow-vests-hails-winds-of-change-idUSKCN1PU25S.

maturing debt in 2019 while still selling long-term debt.[17] This is the equivalent to almost 11% of the total Italian debt burden.

The case of the Italian debt is symptomatic and reflective of the wider problems that the Eurozone is facing. In particular, the efforts to strengthen the foundations of the single currency remain in the forefront of the EU Commission's policy initiatives. However, the progress registered so far based on the "*Five Presidents' Report*"[18] falls short of the one required to ensure the single currency's viability (Commission 2015). The EU Commission identified the main dangers to the single currency and put forward areas required to be addressed.[19] The first threat relates to the economic divergence between the Eurozone core and periphery caused by the debt crisis. This is exacerbated by the economic and financial fragmentation in a number of periphery countries, including Italy, emanating from the high share of NPLs. Second, the threat continues to arise from the rise of populism, with populist parties winning 29% of seats previously 24%, in the recent European elections amounting to 218 of the Parliament's 751 seats. This isn't the expected landslide culminating from debt crises high Eurozone unemployment and mass migration. But populists will be important in voicing their continued hostility to the European project and to Brussels technocrats who they accuse of being deaf to the needs of ordinary citizens.

The ECB's Quantitative Programme (QE) from April 2015 to December 2018 has been crucial in assisting large Eurozone banks in re-building their liquidity and capital ratios from 8.9% in 2010 to approximately 13%. European banks own large amounts of sovereign domestic sovereign debt. For example, Italian lenders hold 387 bn euros. This implies that any spike in the cost of refinancing national debts could translate instantly to a higher cost of finance for domestic banks.

The solution to "breaking" this link is the creation of a comprehensive banking union for the Eurozone. While there has been considerable

---

[17] https://www.bloomberg.com/opinion/articles/2019-02-06/italy-is-playing-with-fire-in-the-bond-markets?srnd=premium-europe.

[18] Ec.europa.eu, 22 June 2015.

[19] https://ec.europa.eu/commission/publications/reflection-paper-deepening-economic-and-monetary-union_en.

progress towards establishing a European banking union, its most crucial element namely a Eurozone (or European) deposit guarantee scheme remains elusive. The Italian debt case is a case in point.

Eurozone periphery countries' authorities are claiming that a Eurozone banking union, including a deposit guarantee scheme, is the only remedy ensuring that speculation would no longer provide a strong incentive for investors and savers to shift part of their liquid assets to other Eurozone countries, in the case of a crisis. Core Eurozone countries led by Germany are opposed to the creation of a European Deposit Insurance Scheme (EDIS)—in other words, an insurance guarantee scheme. The fear is that countries would be less diligent in policing the liquidity of their domestic banks. Stricter regulations are being demanded on bank holdings of sovereign debt before any final decision is made in spite of the efforts of the EU Commission Vice-President, Valdis Dombrovskis. Regarding the capital markets union (CMU), Mr. Dombrovskis suggested there may be delays when he said:

> "What we call for now is that CMU is made a priority, not only in words and political declarations but also in practice, and that tangible progress is made with the legislative proposals that are on the table." Mr. Dombrovskis said.
>
> "It still remains our ambition to have our main building blocks for CMU in place by the end of this mandate," he said, in reference to the end of the commission's term of office in November 2019. "We still think it is realistic but it requires intensive work ... all legislative proposals needed to reach this goal are on the table."

Each perspective involves different policy prescriptions to address the single currency's incomplete nature. These prescriptions are not necessarily mutually exclusive but deviate on the degree to which initiatives should focus on member states' policies or, alternatively, on reviewing EU institutions. Be it as it may, vital questions remain unanswered regarding the legacy of high debts in the EU. For example, have the Eurozone's institutions evolved sufficiently as to be able to withstand the next recession in the EU? Is a fiscal union necessary to ensure the single currency's viability? Is a complete banking union required?

In doing so, it is acknowledged that the overarching framework of the EU features a single currency with immense external potential but internally fragile. The main cause of internal concerns stems from Italy and the country's ability to maintain its fiscal sustainability and social cohesion. Its external potential relates to its legitimate claim of acting as a substitute to the US dollar's major reserve currency status. Each dimension is addressed below, starting from the external one.

In a speech on 28 March 2019, Christine Lagarde, MD International Monetary Fund (IMF), urged Eurozone leaders to make progress on the completion of the CMU when she said:

> But today I *urge* euro area leaders to **reignite the discussion**, to negotiate in good faith and make the difficult compromises, to unlock the full potential of the banking union.[20]

The audience at Banque de France in Paris heard of the need for the completion of the banking union for an integrated single European capital market. With Brexit looming and as yet no firm agreement on level of access to the London capital markets, more diversified sources of financing must be unleashed. Ms. Lagarde highlighted that in the USA, the corporate bond market accounted for more than two-fifths of GDP, compared with only one-tenth in the euro area—and she quoted the former Federal Reserve Chairman Alan Greenspan, who once referred to capital markets as the "*spare tire*" of the financial system.[21] Taking this approach, therefore, would expand the range of domestic and cross-border financing options for European companies and (individual) borrowers heavily reliant at present on (and exposed to) the banking sector for channelling savings and for investment financing. Deposit holders and (bank) shareholders

[20] https://www.imf.org/en/News/Articles/2019/03/28/sp032819-the-euro-area-creating-a-stronger-economic-ecosystem.

[21] Alan Greenspan. (1999). "Do Efficient Financial Markets Mitigate Financial Crises?", Remarks at the 1999 Financial Markets Conference of the Federal Reserve Bank of Atlanta, Sea Island, Georgia.

especially in former *"bailed" out* states like Greece and Cyprus know full well what happens to their savings when their banks defaulted.[22]

The operation of a CMU would introduce a *uniform* cost of funding across EU borders in close geographic proximity.

Is the Euro a Bulwark Against the Dollar? The Euro—A Weapon to Enhance Global Power

The euro is the currency of 19 EU countries (out of 28 member states), and over 340 million of its EU citizens use it daily. Launched on 1 January 1999, it is the second most important currency in the world. With its international role as a unified European currency, the Euro can be an important tool to reinforce Europe globally, to promote its trading interests and influencing global affairs according to rule-based multilateralism. But this is best done in combination with a deep CMU and a pan-Eurozone treasury bond and treasury bills. The CMU project aims to harmonize procedures with the EU to improve cross-border investment despite the fact free movement of capital is part of EU treaty law—ironically a measure that the UK was earlier than most in implementing. But legislation the CMU project is still in the process of completion, delayed by the introduction of policies to simplify bankruptcy proceedings, the development of pan-European pension funds and the creation of a cross-border market in "covered" bonds or debt securities to protect bondholders.

The Current International Role of the Euro

Economic strategy for the Euro has focused almost exclusively on maintaining price stability and fiscal consolidation. In recent years, this has drawn attention on the challenges the currency faced following the

[22] *Cyprus and the Financial Crisis—The Controversial Bailout and What It Means for the Eurozone.* London, Palgrave Macmillan (2015).

financial crash of 2008—and its responses to subsequent crises. But the importance of the Euro goes beyond its internal concerns in playing an important role beyond EU borders the euro area.

As a bloc, the European Union's share of global gross domestic product amounts to an estimated around 17%. The share of the euro area is estimated to be around 12%.[23] It is the second most widely used currency in terms of its share of global payments amounting to around 36% in 2017. By comparison, the US dollar accounts for about 40% of total payments (ECB data from Swift).[24]

The euro can still enhance the resilience of the global financial system by providing market operators across the globe with an additional alternative, especially versus the dollar, and by making the international economy less vulnerable to the shocks that come from so many sectors being reliant on a single global currency—and the US financial systems, institutions and policies underpinning it. The euro has a role in facilitating and expanding Europe's trade agenda, for European companies to trade globally for the benefit of Europe's economy. Sixty other countries and territories around the world, with a population of over 175 million people, utilize the euro as their currency or peg their own currency to it.

The proportion of global holdings of foreign exchange reserves held as Euros currently stands at around 20%. The US dollar's share, by comparison, is over 60%.[25] But no other currency exceeds 5%—safeguarding the European social and regulatory model at home and highlighting its global importance.

The EU is the world's largest trading bloc and the top trading partner of 80 countries across the world. But recent trade wars between USA and China and broader threats to globalized trade patterns from protectionist US policies under the Trump administration will start to require a more robust (international) role for the European Union.

US protectionism, manifesting as it currently is in a war of competing tariffs and counterthreats between the USA and China, affects the

[23]https://ec.europa.eu/info/business-economy-euro/euro-area/international-role-euro_en.

[24]https://ec.europa.eu/commission/news/capital-markets-union-2019-mar-15_en.

[25]B. Eichengreen. (2019). "Two Views of the International Monetary System", *Inter-economics* 54, no. 4, pp. 233–236.

European Union in several ways. First and foremost, it puts at risk multilateralism in trade relations and, in particular, the smooth functioning of the World Trade Organization (WTO). Secondly, it opens the door to additional trade protectionism that could possibly target the EU, which has the world's largest trade surplus.[26] Thirdly, protectionist measures taken by the USA against China—with consequent Chinese retaliation—have indirect consequences for Europe. This can have the positive effect that European exporters have gained a comparative advantage against US exporters in Chinese markets for those US goods on which import tariffs have been imposed and that Europe can itself produce (Wolff 2018). However, this positive scenario is offset by the inherent complexities of global value chains, which can lead to rising costs of production because of third countries' import tariffs that will lie along Europe's supply chain (Chiacchio 2018). This is absolutely the case with China.[27]

US and Iran Sanctions—Implications for the EU

By defaulting on the Joint Comprehensive Plan of Action (JCPA) known as the Iran nuclear framework deal (2015), the Trump administration put at risk its political relations with its closest allies. But worse still came when they (the USA) imposed sanctions on Iran that would apply to foreign companies from other countries that continued to trade with that country.

The US President was able to do this because of the strength of the dollar's international role in international trade and finance. The dollar's international role has been famously called "an exorbitant privilege" by Ben Bernanke (7 January 2016) the former Chairman of the Board of Governors of the Federal Reserve from 2006 to 2014.[28] This enabled the

[26]Struggling trade talks between USA and EU renew the threat of tariffs on European cars.

[27]http://bruegel.org/wp-content/uploads/2019/04/US_China_strategic_competition_EU_080419.pdf.

[28]The term was coined by a former minister of Finance Valery Giscard d'Estaing but it had been referred to by Charles de Gaulle (post-First World War French President) as "Americas first privilege" repeating economist Jacques Rueff.

President to cut off foreign companies' access to US capital markets and dollar transactions—including even most of those that take place outside the USA.

France, Germany and the UK are all co-signatories to the JCPA created Instrument in Support of Trade Exchanges (INSTEX),[29] as a means to protect European companies threatened by US sanctions. But this only demonstrates that the second most powerful currency, the Euro, has no infrastructure empowering it to share at least a portion of the dollar's privilege. Eventually, projects like INSTEX could in turn have an effect on the capacity of the USA to employ sanctions. The diplomacy behind the collapse of the Iran nuclear deal is a test case of the power of modern financial instruments on foreign policy and global geopolitics.

The effectiveness of sanctions per se has often been questioned and for good reason. Take for example those imposed by the EU on Russia for its invasion of Crimea and its proxy war in the Ukraine, but where sanctions have not changed the status quo on the ground—though economically harmful to Russian citizenry. But in sanctions against Iran, the USA has gone a step further by weaponizing the dollar to achieve its foreign policy aims. This may encourage others where possible to create independent financial systems as instruments of policy. INSTEX, essentially a barter scheme, is no substitute. The EU as a major financial player may learn to leverage its influence more effectively in the future and begin to break the hegemony of the dollar.

But still, international European companies simply cannot afford to cut themselves off from dollar markets. The banks lending to them cannot do so either. The stark reality facing the EU is that, for all its financial and economic weight as a single market, it has no effective policy instruments to defend itself against the impact of US sanctions. If the Euro was both a liquid and safe asset, global investors would be able to diversify their dollar holdings to reduce their dependency on the USA. But there is no deep

---

[29] Instrument in support of Trade Exchanges (INSTEX) is essentially a barter system that allows companies in the EU and, potentially elsewhere, to completely avoid the US financial system by eliminating cross-border payments.

European capital market that would allow the EU to retaliate in reciprocal fashion by targeting US companies and banks.[30]

The Euro as a Reserve Currency

One of the arguments in favour of establishing the euro was that it be able to rapidly rival the dollar's status as the global reserve currency and so make it harder for the USA to abuse its "exorbitant privilege".[31] The problem with this strategy is that devaluing the dollar imposes few costs on the USA, because its foreign debt is denominated in dollars (furthermore, US multinational corporations that repatriate a large portion of their earnings from abroad back into the USA can profit off a weak dollar).[32]

There are strong arguments associated with strengthening the role of the Euro in foreign exchange and debt markets, enhancing its ability to compete with the USA's dollar reserve currency status. Recently, this has been encouraged by the absence of any Eurozone bailout programmes and no (immediate) fears concerning a possible collapse of the Eurozone, renewing efforts to promote the Euro's international role and enhancing its reserve status.[33] Reflecting the EU's Commission thinking—and confidence—on the issue Commission President, Jean-Claude Junker, explicitly announced in his State of the Union address on 12 September 2018 that the Commission will present initiatives aiming to boost the international role of the Euro (Efstathiou and Papadia 2018). The EU outlined a two-stage approach, firstly by evaluating the current role of the Euro in international markets and secondly to build deep and liquid European financial markets. Much of the tenor of this strategy was announced by Jean-Claude Junker in his State of the Union address 12 September 2018 to MEPs in Strasberg when he said:

---

30 An additional problem is the EU's large and persistent trade surplus with the rest of the world. Being reliant on others to buy export surpluses and invest your excess savings makes the EU more vulnerable in a conflict.

31 B. Eichengreen. (2019). "Two Views of the International Monetary System", *Inter-economics* 54, no. 4, pp. 233–236.

32 A former US Treasury Secretary, John Connally (in President Nixon's Administration), famously retorted that "the dollar may be our currency, but it's your problem".

33 V. Dendrinou. (2018). "EU Takes on Dollar's Global Dominance in New Push for the Euro".

> It was an "aberration" that the EU paid for more than 80 per cent of its energy imports in US dollars despite only 2 per cent of imports coming from the USA. Most of the dollar-denominated imports are from Russia and the Gulf states.
>
> "We will have to change that. The Euro must become the active instrument of a new sovereign Europe", said Mr. Juncker, whose five-year tenure as Commission President is due to end next year.[34]

His point reflected the fact that the EU's import bill is 300 billion euros when only 2% of its energy came from the USA—a major criticism of the Trump administration levelled at the EU (especially Germany) for its reliance on Russian gas through the Nord Stream 2 project.

The EU's stated intentions to move its energy imports into euros is a development that reflects in part the continuing tensions between the EU and the Trump administration. These initiatives include:

- The Euro's adoption as a default currency in energy contracts between member states and third countries;
- The creation of price benchmarks for crude oil denominated in Euros;
- Rendering hedging euro transactions more attractive.

The Commission's recommendations aim to:

- Reduce the risk of disruptions to energy supplies due to the actions of third countries;
- Reform financial benchmarks, which could also help "increase the attractiveness of trading and pricing euro-denominated instruments";
- Create "a fully integrated instant payment system", to eliminate dependency on foreign providers of card and online payments.

EU Economic Affairs Commissioner Pierre Moscovici went further in saying "A wider use of the euro in the global economy yields important potential for better protecting European citizens and companies against

[34] www.ft.com.

external shocks and making the international finance and monetary system more resilient".[35]

These initiatives, when and if followed through, would help towards a transition to a multipolar international monetary system which includes the USA, Eurozone and China: one that would be far more resilient to financial shockwaves than the current based on the hegemony of the dollar.

There are further advantages to these initiatives. With import and export prices denominated in euros, both the economy and currency would be less vulnerable to the pressures (and, sometimes, shocks) of fluctuating exchange rates. European companies would suffer less exchange rate volatility as well and so be able to operate internationally more easily. Furthermore, as is the case in the USA, the Eurozone would reap the benefit of what are effectively very low interest loans in the form of the substantial central bank holdings of its currency. Finally, the consequent growth of international trade from these policies would boost demand for euros, allowing the Eurozone to very cheaply finance an external deficit—exactly as the USA has been doing for the last few decades.[36]

The EU Economy

The ECB had adopted unconventional monetary policies, with their apogee reached in March 2015 when it committed to its Quantitative Easing, which provided a long-waited vital stimulus to the Eurozone (and wider EU) economy. As a result, during 2015–2018 the EU economy recovered to nominal growth rates of around 2%.

However, despite its overall positive impact, the way Quantitative Easing was implemented suffered from two main drawbacks that limited its effectiveness. First, the ECB purchased Eurozone countries' debt in accordance with their relative GDP and second the fact that the QE's objective was to restore inflation to a target of close to, but still below, 2%.

[35]https://www.bloomberg.com/news/articles/2018-12-05/eu-takes-on-dollar-s-global-dominance-in-new-push-for-euro.

[36]https://www.cer.eu/insights/euro-world%E2%80%99s-reserve-currency.

This led to the very awkward situation where the ECB's QE programme led to purchasing mostly German, French, Italian, Spanish and Dutch debt but limited Irish and Portuguese debt and no Greek debt at all. Given Germany's massive current account surpluses from 2013 to 2017 ranging from 7 to 8% annually, it is really questionable whether the country ever needed to participate in the QE programme, as it was repaying its maturing debt and not issuing new debt, as reflected by the considerable decrease in the German debt-to-GDP ratio down to 68% in 2018.

The QE' objective of restoring inflation to 1.8–1.9% also effectively meant that restoring real growth rates to sustainable levels was not the programme's objective, as was the case with the FED's (Federal Reserve)[37] and the Bank of England's QE programmes. The aim was set in such a way as to incorporate the Northern Eurozone's aversion towards adopting QE and Northern Eurozone countries' consent to allow the ECB to engage in unorthodox monetary policies—but only to a limited extent.[38] One of its side effects was that once inflation was restored to below 2%, the ECB had to halt the programme. This was the case while unemployment rates in the Southern Eurozone remained excessively high and core Eurozone inflation was at 1.5%. The broader negotiating framework in the Eurozone that led to the outcome of the specific type of QE had to reconcile the unabated German fears of de-anchoring inflationary expectations from target and the vital need for higher growth rates in the Eurozone South. It would be interesting to see whether the features of the impending QE programme would deviate significantly from the 2015 to 2018 one.[39]

However, regardless of the specific way QE was conducted the programme achieved one of its broader principles, namely to keep the Eurozone intact. Safeguarding the single currency implied securing Italy's and Spain's (as well as France's) place in it. Given that, the Eurozone debt crisis had the potential to erode Italian and Spanish public finances to such an extent as to endanger the single currency's stability and the absence of the necessary funds to bail out either country (let alone both), implied that ECB's intervention was the only available remedy at the time. From this

[37]The Federal Reserve is the central banking system of the USA.

[38]https://archive.intereconomics.eu/year/2018/3/ecb-quo-vadis/.

[39]*The Economist.* (2019). "The European Central Bank: Space Exploration", 20–26 July, p. 61.

perspective alone, the ECB's QE programme was successful. However, there is only so much QE can do. It effectively bought time for the EU authorities to put in place the missing parts of the Eurozone's architecture namely a pan-Eurozone unemployment insurance scheme, a complete Eurozone banking union and either a fiscal union, or the relaxation of its existing fiscal rules. The new ECB President, Christine Lagarde, will face much more pressure than her predecessor, when the next Eurozone crisis hits, as the re-introduction of QE would not provide a remedy. The considerable reduction in Germany's current account surpluses to below 3% of GDP, in no way reflects the restoration of Eurozone's internal balance as it emanates from reductions in the net volumes of international trade, caused primarily by tariffs imposed by the US administration.

As a result, completing Eurozone's architecture is more essential than ever. However, despite the progress registered, e.g. with establishing the key features of a Eurozone banking union, a complete banking union remains elusive due to the different approaches between the Eurozone "South" and "North". The North, led by Germany, sets a pre-condition for the creation of a complete banking union the return of debt-to-GDP ratios to sustainable levels and the reduction in NPLs. In this way, the creation of a complete Eurozone banking union would not need to bail out collapsing banks in the periphery.[40] On the other hand, South Eurozone countries assert that the delay in creating such a union renders the reduction of debts and NPLs even more difficult. Led by Italy, they claim that the lack of the safety net provided by a deposits guarantee scheme does not eliminate depositors' incentives to shift part of their liquid assets to other Eurozone countries during crises or speculative attacks. This adds more pressure to ailing banks and more difficulty in rescuing them.[41] As both arguments are valid, during the last couple of years, both the North and South Eurozone group of countries have stuck to their guns, with no real progress materializing.

[40] https://www.tandfonline.com/doi/abs/10.1080/09644008.2019.1621296?journalCode=fgrp20.

[41] https://www.tandfonline.com/doi/abs/10.1080/07036337.2019.1622541?journalCode=geui20.

Consequently, the ultimate test for the Eurozone lies ahead. Either the Eurozone North countries adhere to pro-growth policies by, for example, accepting a temporary deviation from inflation target and some form of relaxing the Euro's fiscal rules *or* they will have to face the consequences of a "big" Eurozone country departing from the single currency. In the meantime, the Eurozone will keep experiencing the same repercussions emanating from negative real interest rates as the UK, albeit not to the same extent.

3

Immigration: What Now?

Distinctions between EU and non-EU migration. The lessons of Brexit; Britain's EU citizens deal reciprocity. Survival of Schengen and solutions to mass migration.

Migration—History of *Intra*-EU Mobility

Historically, economic migration from *within* Europe is nothing new. The origins of free movement stem from the post-war need to encourage rapid economic growth after the devastation of Europe's industrial sector, towns and cities. This could only be attained by encouraging policies of flexible mobility of qualified and skilled workers throughout the EEC, the forerunner of the European Community and the EU. Between 1958 and 1972, work permits were granted to what were colloquially known as "gasterbeiters" or "guest workers" in the Benelux countries of Belgium,

J. Theodore, *Survival of the European (Dis) Union*,
https://doi.org/10.1007/978-3-030-31214-5_3

Netherlands and Luxembourg, France, Italy and West Germany (the Federal Republic of Germany)[1] Similar schemes operated in the Scandinavian countries.

About 30% of these foreign workers came from what was then referred to as the European Economic Community (the EEC); from the high unemployment regions of southern Italy, Greece and Spain; but also, in substantial numbers, from Turkey, a country outside the EEC. The latter have moved almost exclusively to Germany's industrial heartlands, with most remaining to this day.[2]

With the continuing enlargement process from the 1980s, the operation of transitional restrictions on free movement for new members helped to quell concerns that immediate freedom of movement would lead to mass migration (notably, Britain waved these controls under the Blair-Brown governments).[3] But with EU enlargement from Central and Eastern Europe fears resurfaced of an exodus of large numbers of migrant workers seeking employment opportunities in the west.

Current EU members shouldn't need reminding that they already signed up to this principle of the *single market*, namely freedom of movement (FOM), albeit not foreseeing the extent of such an enlargement that has now driven to the very geographical borders of Europe. Clearly, the right to free movement is enshrined in the founding Treaty of Rome 1957 that established the European Economic Community (EEC), and will unquestionably remain. The intent and consequence of this policy were that the very borders that had been fought over in two world wars were now permanently open for Europeans to conduct trade through the free movement of capital, labour and services.[4]

In May 2004, the 15 states of the European Union were joined by ten new member states in what was the largest expansion in the history of European economic integration. The new member states included Czech

---

[1]West Germany signed bilateral agreements with a number of European countries (Italy, Greece and Spain) and Turkey which allowed for the recruitment of less skilled workers in West Germany's factories during the boom years of industrial growth known at the time as the German "Economic Miracle".

[2]Those from Algeria went to France and the UK continued to receive many from the British Commonwealth.

[3]For Greece (1981) and Spain and Portugal (1986), there was a 6-year transitional period.

[4]Freedom of Movement was one of the original Four 'Freedoms' with Capital, Customs and Services.

Republic, Hungary, Poland, Slovakia, Slovenia and the three Baltic states of Estonia, Latvia and Lithuania. Cyprus and Malta also acceded at the same time. But unlike in the 1980s, when Greece, Spain and Portugal had joined, significant fears existed of mass migration from these new East European accession states based on the much great disparity in incomes and living standards enjoyed by their workers over those in the west. Consequently, the accession of the new members was coupled with the imposition of a seven-year transition period to try (somewhat unsuccessfully) and mute this impact.

Only the UK, Sweden, Ireland and Malta allowed citizens from these new accession countries to work in their labour markets immediately, which led to sizeable inflows (the largest of the new accession countries) into these countries, particularly Poland.[5] Since its accession to the EU in 2004, and the Schengen area in particular, around two million Poles have emigrated—primarily to the UK, Ireland and Germany. The majority, according to the Central Statistical Office of Poland, left seeking higher wages abroad, while retaining full residency status in their home country.[6]

It is estimated that between 2004 and 2008, Poland's net outflow of over 380,000 citizens accounted for about 1% of its total population. The substantial increase in this outflow, in that nation and throughout Eastern Europe, has led to concerns by their authorities of a serious "brain drain" from the very countries most in need of such skilled professionals—trained at their own government's expense in *their* universities. As an example, 8896 Polish medical staff are now in service in the UK National Health Service (NHS) and 1633 doctors registered between 2004 and 2007[7] although Brexit will influence future migration. The NHS as an institution now has over a quarter of the doctors who are not of British national origin.[8] This development sits ill at ease with the original purpose

[5]UK choose not to use this option at all, when the Czech Republic, Estonia, Hungary, Latvia, Lithuania, Poland, Slovakia and Slovenia joined. The UK was one of only 3 of the original EU members (UK, Sweden and Eire) to choose not to apply transitional restrictions on these eight countries.

[6]Anne White. (2011). "Post-communist Poland: Social Change and Migration", in *Polish Families and Migration Since EU Accession*. Policy Press. p. 27.

[7]www.lse.ac.uk/eurohealth/Lesniowska.

[8]Including those from outside the EU.

of the enlargement—which was, and still is, to develop economies of the poorer members of the EU.[9]

Immigration at the time of this enlargement time was not perceived as such a significant threat in these countries—in contrast to France, where a fictional character iconized as the "Polish Plumber" was used to fuel fears on how skilled French workers were soon to be replaced by a flood of cheap Eastern European labour. Around 70% of migrants from the post-2004 accession states have gone to Ireland and the UK. Migrants from Bulgaria and Romania, conversely, have mostly chosen to go to Italy and Spain (in the case of Romania, linguistic affinity in a Romance language appears to have played a part).

Freedom of Movement (FOM) and Fears Raised in the UK Referendum Campaign

Controlling intra-EU migration was the defining election campaign issue in the 2016 UK referendum campaign. It reflected widespread opposition to EU migration fuelled by the massive 2015 influx of Syrian refugees to Germany. Viewed by many a necessary humanitarian act, it caused antagonism particularly in Hungary and Poland fearing it to be part of a future trend of mass migration. Leave campaigners Nigel Farage of UKIP and Boris Johnson played on voters fears. In Boris Johnson's case, he suggested (since denied) that Turkey's accession to the EU could flood the country with up to 77 million migrants. In April 2016, Johnson warned: "I am very pro-Turkish but what I certainly can't imagine is a situation in which 77 million of my fellow Turks and those of Turkish origin can come here without any checks at all. That is mad – that won't work". In a joint statement with Michael Gove, fellow Brexiteer, which was sent (just before the referendum) to Prime Minister David Cameron, they stated: "*Despite the rapidly accelerating pace of accession negotiations, 'In' campaigners maintain that* Turkey 'is not an issue in this referendum and it shouldn't be'"; the statement went on to say:

---

[9] 63,000 NHS staff in England are EU nationals House of Commons library published 10 October 2018.

> Others assert that the UK has 'a veto' on Turkish accession. This claim is obviously artificial given the government's commitment to Turkish accession at the earliest possible opportunity.
>
> If the government cannot give this guarantee, the public will draw the reasonable conclusion that the only way to avoid having common borders with Turkey is to vote Leave and take back control on 23 June.[10]

Immigration had dominated the outcome of many local and national elections and was a key factor in the upsurge of the UK Independence Party (UKIP), which was able to pull in popular support from both left and right by courting the anti-immigration, anti-EU as well as the anti-establishment vote. In doing so, it attracted five million votes in the last UK general election in May 2015—though under the British first-past-the-post-electoral system, this gave it only a single seat. "There are of course different views on how important the role of immigration in the 2016 referendum played in the Leave vote overall. Even the aspects that were about EU immigration did not necessarily come from people directly affected by it. For some it could be the perception of it happening and the failure of government to manage migration. This became part of a national narrative that people have come in to take away jobs and were changing aspects of British life." [11]

Highly politicized figures supplied to Parliament forecasted that up to three million more migrants could arrive in the UK by 2030.[12] It is statistics like this that gave ammunition to the Leave campaign. Arguments put forward by government and think tanks claiming that immigration is good for the country only alienated voters in the depressed post-industrial towns and cities of north-east England. A counter-argument was put forward by local and regional authorities, including town and city councils, that high net immigration put greater burden on the provision of local services and infrastructure—especially housing—at a time of austerity,

---

[10] https://www.independent.co.uk/news/uk/politics/boris-johnson-brexit-turkey-eu-referendum-vote-leave-campaign-michael-gove-a8734296.html.

[11] An interview (personal views) with Anna Mikhailova Political Correspondent for the *Daily Telegraph*.

[12] https://hansard.parliament.uk/Commons/2016-05-05/debates/16050510800002/EUImmigration.

an acute housing crisis and cutbacks in local services by central government. Economic data showed that immigration—especially highly skilled immigrants—was a spur to economic growth and created more than 2 million jobs since 2005 fell on deaf ears with the majority of the electorate.[13]

The Blair government post-2004 clearly underestimated the level of economic migrants from the EU accession states. Today, net migration of EU migrants to the UK has dropped to its lowest level since 2009. Central and Eastern European citizens have in some cases chosen to leave. The level of uncertainty on EU citizens' rights still remains an issue even though it remains part of the EU–UK Withdrawal Agreement of 14 November. Others have been deterred by the weakness of the pound during 3 years of protracted Brexit negotiations and by better prospects for work and higher wage growth in their home country.

Immigration expert, Madeleine Sumption, the director of the Migration Observatory at the University of Oxford, has said:

> The overall story the data tell on EU migration is clear. Britain is not as attractive to EU migrants as it was a couple of years ago.
>
> EU net migration happened to be unusually high in the run-up to the referendum, so at least some of this decline would probably have happened anyway, even without Brexit.[14]

Limits on Freedom of Movement

The issues around freedom of movement (FOM) will continue to haunt post-Brexit governments.[15] British industry, the National Health Service

---

[13]OECD April 2016 controversial report entitled "The Economic Consequences of Brexit: A Taxing Decision" suggested that a Brexit vote would be damaging to the UK with a "knock on" effect on other European countries and also reducing the UK GDP by over 3% by 2020 and 5% by 2030. The report forecasts a decline in foreign direct investment, as the UK would no longer be the conduit allowing for access to the EU internal market. See also the (NIESR) National Institute of Economic and Social Research report to be published 9 May 2016.

[14]*Guardian*, 28 February 2019.

[15]See Chapter 4 on Populism and the aftermath of Brexit.

(NHS) and the Food and Agricultural sectors all have severe staff shortages which cannot be filled by the domestic labour market alone. Non-EU workers will have to fill these vacancies if restrictions for EU citizens remain government policy in the future. The Remain campaign in 2016 failed to explain that EU law never guaranteed an absolute right to move and reside anywhere in the EU. Treaty rights of free movement are subject to limitations. Article 45(3) of the Treaty on the Functioning of the European Union (TFEU) states:

> that the rights to (a) accept offers of employment, (b) move freely between States to take up employment, (c) reside in other Member States, and (d) the right to stay in another Member State after employment has finished, are subject to 'limitations justified on grounds of public policy, public security or public health'.[16]
>
> Article 45(4) TFEU adds a further exception – that the free movement provisions shall not apply to employment in the public service, so that where roles are thought to be nationally sensitive, involving participation in the exercise of powers conferred by public law and duties designed to safeguard the general interests of the State, they may be reserved for nationals.[17]

It is clear that little attempt (by politicians) was made to explain to the British electorate that national governments had the ability to adopt restrictive measures on the grounds set out above. The UK had not registered migrants as they arrive and so had no way of knowing how long they had been in the country since no effort was made to track or control this movement. This provided further ammunition to the Eurosceptic cause who was able to depict freedom of movement as "uncontrolled migration".[18]

---

[16]Article 45(3) of the Treaty on the Functioning of the European Union (TFEU).

[17]Article 45(4) of the Treaty on the Functioning of the European Union (TFEU).

[18]The UK government reintroduced exit checks in 2015, but these fell well short of the physical, visible checks after security, which are airport-enforced.

Freedom of Movement—Protecting the Rights of EU Citizens

The UK government's long drawn-out negotiations with the EU produced a Withdrawal Agreement[19] (and Political Declaration) more commonly referred to as *Theresa May's deal* which failed to get parliamentary approval on three occasions.

The agreement with the EU included the safeguarding of EU citizens' rights in the UK post-Brexit. There was cross-party consensus for this even among Leave voters in the 2016 referendum. Despite this, many uncertainties remain principally on complex bureaucratic procedures for securing residency rights or "settled Status".

The New Immigration Regime—Search for Skilled Workers

The UK government is unable to stem the outflow of highly skilled workers—including scientists, academics and entrepreneurs now leaving, with far fewer replacements coming to fill their places. For employers, the situation looks bleak if, as is thought, a new visa system starts to put "Britain first"—by focusing on training UK workers rather than engaging people from abroad—a process that may take some time to implement. Hristriana Georgieva a foreign-born entrepreneur and British passport holder has witnessed the difficulty facing even highly skilled EU nationals since the 2016 referendum. "People who came to the UK with high hopes and who are proud to make a contribution economically feel like strangers in their adopted country. It will be a mistake to lose them".[20]

Employers in industries such as agriculture, hospitality and the leisure—which rely on low-skilled seasonal workers—would be worst hit by any future immigration regime, because it would make it harder for all but the most high-skilled migrants to enter the UK. The NHS has seen a substantial drop (89%) in EU nationals joining the nursing profession

[19]The Draft Agreement on the Withdrawal of the United Kingdom from the European Union published on 14 November 2018 on how to implement Brexit.

[20]Interview held on 20 July 2019.

in the year up to September 2017, with 69% also leaving over the same period.

The National Farmers Union (NFU) has reported that a shortage of labour is leaving fruit and vegetables unharvested, and has requested that the government respond effectively by putting in place an agricultural workers scheme in place. East European workers already find the UK less attractive as a result of the falling value of the pound.

The UK government through its EU Settlement Scheme is at last giving recognition for the need to halt the outflow of EU citizens. Over 400,000 European nationals have applied to secure their stay/to remain in the UK after Brexit, and the application process is open until 30 June 2021. This concern was amplified in a statement by the British Home Secretary, Sajid Javid, when he said: "EU citizens have contributed so much to this country and we want them all to stay. That's why we have made the EU settlement scheme free and simple to use. It's vital no one is left behind and we support vulnerable people who may have difficulties applying. This £9 million of funding will help do that".[21] The settlement scheme is open to citizens of EU member states plus those from Iceland, Liechtenstein, Norway and Switzerland, as well as their family members. Successful applicants are granted immigration status confirming their right to continue living and working in the UK indefinitely.

Under the EU Settlement Scheme, you'll continue to have the right to live and work in the UK. It means you'll continue to be eligible for public services, such as healthcare and schools' public funds and pensions.

Some EU citizens, led by UK-based Poles, are objecting to the application process under the EU Settlement Scheme as a means of protecting existing rights currently enjoyed. Many have signed a petition (deadline for signature by 13 November 2019) launched by Damian Wawrzyniak, a Polish chef who has appeared on TV with Mary Berry and James Oliver. He has challenged the UK government and Parliament website to change the wording of the settlement status process from "application" to "registration". Wawrzyniak is typical of EU citizens such as Elwira Debicka who says: "I have lived in the UK for many years and enjoyed my time here and do hope that if I register I am free to continue to have rights to

[21] www.theguardian.com, 10 April 2019.

work and to return to the UK if for any reason I decide to live and/or work outside the UK for any period. This is what I think a lot of EU citizens in the UK will also be thinking about and I am sure this will be the case".

UK Expatriates—To What Extent Are Their Rights Preserved Post-Brexit

The currently unratified EU–UK Withdrawal Agreement incorporates detailed protection for EU citizens. Reciprocal arrangements will apply for UK expatriates as in theory, most EU countries were not calling into question the rights of Britons living in the EU. But understandably, many expatriates felt and still feel uncertain as to whether they are allowed to retain their EU citizenship and especially the rights and benefits that go with continued EU citizenship—including the right to travel, live, study and work wherever they choose in the EU. They would also expect to be in receipt of a wide range of other additional rights regarding health, education, work and social security. The continued provision of health care (and reciprocal arrangements) has been of particular concern for those living in retirement on the Mediterranean littoral.

But not all aspects of FoM were universally accepted. Some EU member states, in contrast, had been more proactive than the UK when interpreting EU law on freedom of movement. These countries recognized opportunities for effectively exercising more "control of our borders". This included registering migrants as they arrived, as Germany did, and the imposition of time limits on any stay without gaining employment, as was the case in Belgium where migrants *must* register within 3 months with the local authorities, and if they intend to work, their claim will be assessed and processed within six months.[22]

[22] Directive 2004/38/EC (the "EU citizens' Directive", which is the source of the main legal rules on this issue) sets out the "categories" of people with an EU law-based right to reside in a host Member State for longer than three months—essentially, workers/the self-employed and their family members, students and the self-sufficient. Students must have health insurance and make a declaration of sufficient resources.

Posted Workers Directive—Opposition Within the EU

The system of posting workers abroad—a scheme governed by the Posted Workers Directive[23] on home wages and conditions—aroused particular hostility in France with litigation against companies in the French courts. In October 2014, a French court ruled that Ryanair had to pay €8.3 million (£7.6 million), stating that it had broken local labour laws by employing over 120 staff on Irish contracts in Marseille.[24] France, under newly elected President Macron, led the opposition to the EU's Posted Workers Directive. Macron had demanded an end to what he called "social dumping", by saying that: "'social dumping' of cheap migrant workers puts the whole EU at risk".

The Posted Workers Directive scheme had permitted companies to send their cheaper workers to other EU states but keeping them on existing employment terms which undercut wages and working conditions in higher wage countries. In 2018, Macron obtained wide support from EU partners (with the main exception of Poland) to limit "postings" to 6 months instead of the original 12 months. The reforms also required employers to adhere to local employment laws including the provision of local holidays and insurance entitlements. It was fortunate that to become law provided it had EU parliamentary approval, the revised Posted Workers Directive adopted on 28 June 2018 required only a qualified majority vote in the EU Council—not the support of all 28 nations.

---

[23]A posted worker is defined as "a person who, for a limited period of time, carries out his or her work in the territory of an EU Member State other than the state in which he or she normally works" (Council Directive 96/71/EC). Directive 96/71 only takes employees into consideration.

[24]*BBC News*, 24 August 2017.

Non-EU Migration: The Search for a Solution

Causes of Non-EU Migration

Migration into the EU is not simply a consequence of recent wars in the Middle East, or the ongoing economic plight of Africa.[25] It is also closely linked to broader processes of globalization. As a result of the proliferation of the Internet throughout the third world—up from 9% in 2006 to 32% in 2014[26]—driven by the exponential adoption of smartphones since 2007, the world's poorest citizens can now receive a much better picture of the economic opportunities, or necessities, present in the richer nations of the first world. Migrants do not have to be in war-torn Syria or eking out an existence in "no go" areas in downtown Bagdad or Mogadishu. And typically, they no longer have faith in their country's ability to stabilize civil disorder, still less raise living standards and economic well-being. But still it was the mass migration of Syrian refugees in July 2015 which provided the wakeup call for Brussels to address the immediate disastrous humanitarian crisis—shouldered by Germany in the first instance but which faced growing opposition to any EU-wide sharing of the growing burden of essentially Muslim immigrants from war-torn regions.

Brussels Imposition of Refugee Quotas

Both Hungary and Poland were in the vanguard of those countries alarmed by the dramatic influx of new Muslims into Europe. There was widespread fear this new wave of Muslim refugees represented conservative societies with backgrounds that would bring about a radical change to their nation's social demographics. Their reluctance to take in Syrian refugees revolved around worries, fair or unfair, about the integration of potentially enormous numbers of ethnically, religiously, culturally and linguistically diverse and different migrants. Reactions by opponents to this influx have

[25]The destruction of the Gaddafi regime in 2011 engineered (in part) by the West, leaving anarchy to reign in Libya coupled with the failure to act decisively to intervene in Syria's civil war created the conditions for the mass migrations now destabilizing the EU.

[26]Data published by the Internal Telecommunications Union, published 25 May 2015.

oscillated between the religious and the economic. In the Netherlands, the Geert Wilders, a Dutch right-wing politician, called the immigrant surge an "Islamic invasion", one that "threatens our prosperity, our security, our culture and identity".[27] In August 2015, the Slovak government said it would only accept Christians from Syria because "in Slovakia we don't have mosques", according to an interior department spokesman.[28] In Poland, things went a step further as the authorities required that verification of "Christian" status would have to be certified by clergy at home. Former French President Nicolas Sarkozy focused instead on economic factors, describing as "folly" the idea of "taking on dozens of thousands of migrants for whom we have no jobs in Europe". With an unemployment rate of over 10%, France already has experienced significant problems with the assimilation of Muslim migrants since its colonial control of North Africa. Terrorism and security issues in post-2016 alienated French society even more providing ammunition for Jean-Marie Le Pen's National Rally party (formerly the National Front).

Subsequent events and the rising tide of anti-EU and anti-immigrant populism across the continent have made it clear the problems of migration pose the greatest challenge and potential existential threat to the stability of the European project. It concerns the entire EU membership and not just the Eurozone. It has and continues to stir more anti-EU sentiment than the ongoing debt crisis, even in countries with less of a Eurosceptic electorate. It continues to be a threat to EU solidarity if left unresolved. As previously discussed, in the UK, it became the central theme of the proponents of the Brexit Leave campaign and was ruthlessly exploited by UKIP in their referendum "Leave" campaign. When linked to the inflow of refugees and economic migrants from outside the EU, it has been one of the main reasons for the growth of right-wing parties in Europe particularly in Germany, France, the Netherlands and among most of the post-2004 accession states of Central and Eastern Europe.[29] Hostile voters, and their

[27] http://www.reuters.com/article/us-europe-migrants-netherlands-idUSKCN0RA0WY20150910.

[28] At the Bratislava EU Summit 16 September 2016, hosted by the Slovakia, the Visegrad Group called for "flexible solidarity", a policy by which states that do not want to take migrants could contribute financially with equipment and manpower to the EU's migration policy—as is already the case in the Balkans.

[29] COR interviews and Polish commentators.

self-appointed representatives on both left and right, claimed that it took away jobs and imposed strains on housing, welfare, education and health care: strains felt hardest among the poor. Anti-immigration became the main battle cry of populist movements throughout the EU prompting action at the very heart of the Brussels establishment.

Germany not Immune from the Backlash

Many of the EU citizens opposed to the massive influx of refugees came from within Germany itself. At the time, Merkel and her Christian Democratic Party (CDU) had no mandate from the German electorate. Arguments that Germany still had strong economic and demographic growth, so could successfully absorb this influx, at least in economic terms did not wash with the German electorate. But even in 2015 this was clearly no longer the case. While German unemployment appeared low (4.7%), the economy was only growing at 1.6% annually. German research institutes including the Ifo (Munich) have now slashed growth forecasts to 0.8% for 2019 although growth projections for 2020 are 1.8%.[30] For the rest of Europe, the ability to absorb a refugee influx is made even worse with falling productivity and high youth unemployment. Current global trade disputes and the fallout from a disorderly Brexit will tarnish this outlook.

Does Migration Help Germany?

Reasons other than altruism may well have influenced Germany's elite to push for what was an unpopular and an ill-conceived policy decision. Reparations for the guilt of its Nazi past are cited but more relevant for welcoming an influx of refugees is to meet the future needs of its workforce as Germany has the world's lowest birth rate. According to current demographic estimates, the population of 81 million today will shrink to 68 million in a few decades. "What Germany is proposing", said syndicated columnist Rich Lowry, "is undertaking a vast social and demographic experiment, with the rapid, bulk importation of Muslim

[30]http://www.bloomberg.com/2019-04-04.

immigrants into a country with an aging population" ("The Refugee Crisis Is Exposing Europe's Folly", *New York Post*, 8 September 2015). In his book *the Strange Death of Europe*, Douglas Murray[31] argues that, instead of importing young people, European governments should first "work out whether there are policies that could encourage more procreation among their existing populations" a suggestion that is currently being eagerly taken up by both right-wing governments in Hungary and Poland by providing financial incentives to families to have more children. The Hungarian PM Viktor Orban extended a lifetime tax exemption for all Hungarian women who had four children in an effort to stem the country's falling birth rate and acute labour shortages partly due to emigration of the skilled workers.

> "There are fewer and fewer children born in Europe," Mr Orban stated in his annual State of the Nation address. "For the west, the answer is immigration. For every missing child there should be one coming in and then the numbers will be fine. But we do not need numbers. We need Hungarian children."[32]

Opposition to Brussels Imposed Refugee Quotas

The immediate response by the EU Commission was to spread the misery and impose refugee quotas on all EU member states provoking an immediate backlash. Opposition was especially felt in post-2004 EU accession states notably Hungary and Poland. But other EU members were united against imposed quotas as George Shishkov, a former Bulgarian MP, pointed out that this was directed at economic migrants "whereas refugees were always welcome".[33] But in effect no government in the EU block was spared the wrath of anti-immigration hostility. In Germany, the political change in climate towards continued acceptance and integration

[31] Douglas Murray, The Strange Death of Europe Published by Bloomsbury 2017.

[32] *Financial Times*, 10 February 2019.

[33] Interview held on 17 June 2019 with George Shishkov a former MP Bulgarian of the Democratic party and Presidential Adviser on Border Control and Frontex Operations in Bulgaria.

of large numbers of refugees—including those that fall under the heading of "economic migrants"—was influenced by a number of events. The shift in attitude crystalized German public opinion in the much publicized Cologne riots. These occurred on New Year's Eve, 2015, when the police recorded 553 criminal complaints by women—of which 45% related to sexual attacks by gangs of North African/Arab men. This provided strong ammunition for more right-wing protesters who blame these violations on the large influx of refugees in 2015. But the main backlash came on 12 January 2016 in Leipzig, Eastern Germany, when the police arrested right-wing anti-migrant demonstrators reacting to the events in Cologne.[34] It was these events that provided the impetus and raison d'etre for a surge of the right-wing opposition. It led to the success of the Alternative fur Deutschland (AFD) in the German federal elections in September 2017 gaining 94 seats representing 12.6% of the vote providing the foundations for the surge of populism throughout Europe.

Terrorism and Security Issues

Exacerbating the formidable challenge Europe has been facing in the migration crisis is the growing security threats to its citizens from terror attacks, such as the coordinated bombings in Paris on 13 November 2015, killing 130, and Brussels in March 2016, which left 31 dead. (The group calling itself Islamic State (ISIL) admitted responsibility in both cases.) What made the attacks particularly alarming in the context of border security is that the terrorists had been able to re-enter the EU in the guise of refugees, as border controls do not track their movements back across the EU's external entry points from the training camps in Syria, Iraq and elsewhere.[35]

As state authorities are pledged first and foremost to protect their citizens, the very freedoms upon which the EU was established have been increasingly placed under threat. Freedom of movement and travel, cornerstone principles of the EU, coupled with the right to privacy and freedom

[34]https://www.ft.com/content/7728b140-b90a-11e5-b151-8e15c9a029fb.

[35]The EU has announced tighter control for ID cards in order to reduce identity fraud 21 February 2019.

from surveillance are challenged by these fears. Increasing the powers of the police and security services may, at least in the short term, help to counter this rising external threat. Investigation has shown that cross-border sharing of intelligence has not been effective and that improving and streamlining these channels through organs such as Interpol are vital to dealing with the problem in future.[36] This has surfaced prominently in the UK–EU Brexit negotiations with the British government giving assurances that any future relationship should maintain the closest cooperation on security matters.[37]

"Our security relationships are unconditional with our European colleagues… We need each other. This is a two-way street and that isn't going to change", Alex Younger, the head of the MI6 foreign intelligence service, told Reuters in an interview earlier on Friday.

"The relationship that exists between us and our European partners is closer than I have ever known it in my 30 years as an intelligence officer. Brexit doesn't fundamentally alter those relationships", he said.[38]

Owing to recent terrorist attacks, the EU' "open borders" policy enshrined in the EU Schengen Agreement[39] has in recent years come into disrepute. But it does have some important caveats. The treaty does permit signatory states to control borders in situations of "national security", or for matters more vaguely defined as "public policy". The regulations were partly suspended during the worst of the crisis in August 2015 when the Merkel government in Germany made use of the "sovereignty clause" to take on a special responsibility for processing applications for Syrian asylum refugees.[40] This was followed by the Czech government in

[36]http://www.telegraph.co.uk/news/2016/03/23/european-cross-border-security-years-away-experts-warn/.

[37]https://www.statewatch.org/news/sep, 14 September 2018.

[38]https://uk.reuters.com/article/uk-germany-security-britain-intelligence/brexit-wont-deter-european-security-cooperation-intelligence-chiefs-idUKKCN1Q41RW.

[39]Schengen Agreement is a treaty which led to the creation of Europe's Schengen Area, in which internal border checks have largely been abolished. It was signed on 14 June 1985, near the town of Schengen, Luxembourg, by five of the ten member states of the then European Economic Community. There are currently 26 members (the UK and Ireland are not members).

[40]George Shishkov formerly head of Bulgaria's Border Control recommends strengthening of Frontex the EU agency charged with management of Schengen and EU external borders (interview 17 June 2019).

September, who also agreed that Syrian refugees could have their applications processed in the Czech Republic, even though they had applied for asylum in other EU countries.

In today's crises, the burden of conducting this rests on those countries with external EU borders through the Mediterranean; this overwhelmingly means Greece and Italy, with Greece, pivoted at the edge of Europe, carrying the greatest toll in terms of sheer numbers.[41] But in a report on the functioning of the Schengen, MEPs warn that the passport-free area is under "enormous pressure". This view was contained in a report authored by Carlos Coelho, a Portuguese member of the EPP group, who said: "National governments made Schengen into the scapegoat of the failures of security policies and of the weakness of common European asylum system. Yet, Schengen is not the problem, it is the solution".[42] Coelho had warned that rhetoric of blaming free movement could destroy the unique Schengen system: "If Schengen perishes, the Europe of citizens that we have today will vanish".

Stemming the Flow of Non-EU Migrants Status of the EU–Turkey Agreement

Positive action by Brussels to placate the mounting resentment of EU governments came with the EU's hasty agreement with Turkey on 18 March 2016. It was by far the most important arrangement for stemming the flow of refugees through Europe's south-eastern underbelly/flank still in operation today. It was a determined plan to return all new arrivals from Turkey to Greece with the Ankara government agreeing also to prevent new land and sea routes. The arrangement led to a significant reduction in the numbers of refugees arriving in Greece from Turkey. For Chancellor

41 In 2008, the Italian and Libyan governments agreed a treaty to stop uncontrolled migration from Libya To Italy which led to the enforced return of migrants by the Italian coast guard authorities, a policy which fell apart with the advent of civil war against the Gaddafi regime in 2011 but which also led to a ruling by the European Court of Human Rights in 2012 that Italy was in breach of the European Convention of Human rights for expelling migrants to face potential danger from the regime in Libya.

42 www.europarl.europa.eu/eu-affairs/sc..., 29 May 2018.

Merkel of Germany, it was important to achieve the deal with Turkey's President Erdogan who agreed to take back Syrian migrants reaching Greece illegally, via the Aegean Islands. In return, Merkel accepted the planned relocation in Europe of Syrian refugees now in camps in Turkey. As a quid pro quo, Turkey was to receive €3 billion to help with the crisis and also a promise by Chancellor Merkel—following her meeting with Recep Tayyip Erdogan the Turkish President (and Prime Minister Ahmet Davutoglu), to progress Turkey's application to join the EU.[43] As a gesture of goodwill, she had also promised to offer Germany's support to speed up plans to ease visa restrictions for Turkish citizens to visit the EU (within the Schengen area), a promise the EU has yet still to fulfil.[44] However, progress continues to be made in the resettlement programme for Syrian refugees.[45]

The EU's Future Approach to Migration

By the middle of 2018, the number of migrants arriving in Europe had fallen by up to 90% since their peak in 2015. But this was not enough to assuage public opinion still hostile to continued migration. On 28 and 29 June, the EU heads of government met in Brussels to address their responses to the latest trade tensions, external migration and security issues affecting the bloc.[46] The agenda was dominated by the political strains facing Chancellor Merkel and her coalition partner—the Bavarian Christian Social Union, CSU party led by Horst Seehofer demanding reform of Europe's migration issues and policies. Fearful of losing further ground

---

[43] EU leaders views on Turkish visas and Acqui Communitaire progression.

[44] https://www.aa.com.tr/europe/Merkel-....

[45] **EU Support to Syrian Refugees in Turkey**

The EU is supporting refugees in Turkey with €6 billion for 2016-2019 through its Facility for Refugees in Turkey—€3 billion from the EU budget and €3 billion contributed by EU Member States—in two tranches. By the end of 2017, the EU had fully committed and contracted €3 billion under the first tranche with 72 projects rolled out, showing tangible results, with more than €2 billion disbursed. The EU is currently mobilizing the second tranche of facility funding and has already committed €1.2 billion, of which €450 million has been contracted and €150 million disbursed. Facility funding goes to projects to address the needs of refugees and host communities with a focus on humanitarian aid, education, health, and socioeconomic support that includes the necessary municipal infrastructure.

[46] "The EU's migration policy must be linked to Security, stronger security reinforced by technological advances" (George Shishkov former Head of Border control in Bulgaria).

to the AFD, Seehofer threatened closure of Germany's borders with Austria and Italy to asylum seekers but by the morning of 29 June 2018, a compromise agreement had averted the collapse of Merkel's coalition. The controversial issue of refugee quotas was carefully avoided. Italy's new populist coalition government accepted a proposal, rescued migrants would in future be sent to Euro-wide "controlled centres"—an idea first proposed by France and Spain, but then only on a voluntary basis. This decision had to accommodate the hostility of the EU's populist governments to any Brussels' imposed compulsory arrangements—not least the new Italian coalition in power on an anti-immigration platform and aligned with the mood in Central Europe.[47]

The New Pragmatism

Merkel recognized the necessity for better regulation: "We must have more regulation regarding every type of migration, so that people have the impression that law and order are being enforced but emphasizing migration was a 'global problem requiring a global solution'". "How we deal with the migrant question will decide whether Europe continues to exist in the future", she said, referring to her fraught attempts to secure deals with other EU members to accept the return of refugees who had registered in their countries.[48] However, she also outlined what she believed to be the necessity of protecting Europe's outer borders more effectively, a policy which involved agreeing partnerships with African countries to tackle illegal migration and lessen the incentives for economic migration. All this required a robust strategy not only for Europe but also for all developed democracies. The immigration summit was able to present a united front and to avoid what could become a force for (EU) disintegration. In a spirit of cooperation, Spain and Greece—as countries of "first arrival"—both entered a trilateral agreement with Germany for the return of refugees to be processed on this basis.

---

[47] Italy has refused to take in people from search-and-rescue ships since its government came to office last June. The country's deputy Prime Minister, Matteo Salvini, has declared Italian waters closed to rescue boats, leaving a series of NGO vessels and their stricken passengers stuck at sea with nowhere to land.

[48] www.theguardian.com, 4 July 2018.

The new pragmatism has its critics.[49] The EU mandate of EUNAVFOR MED Operation Sophia was to stop (on 31 March 2019) the sea patrols that had rescued thousands of refugees and migrants from the Central Mediterranean, despite the threats from Italy's populist government to veto the whole operation.[50] A spokeswoman for the EU's foreign policy chief, Federica Mogherini, acknowledged that Operation Sophia needed substantial numbers of boats to be truly effective. "Operation Sophia is an essential part of the European Union's work to dismantle the business model of traffickers and improve the overall maritime security and stability in the central Mediterranean", she said.[51] The international aid group Médecins Sans Frontières (MSF) was more scathing describing the decision to halt Operation Sophia as "irresponsible and reckless".

This policy change came despite the growth of failed states in Africa, the chaos in Libya and Syria. For Brussels, the priority lay in the management of migration remaining as important as Eurozone reform for the future stability of the EU project. It needed the support of the new Italian ruling alliance. Matteo Salvini, Italy's interior minister and fierce critic of years of mass migration, believed some "real progress" had been made.

Support for Merkel also came from an unlikely quarter: Premier Alexis Tsipras, who had just rehabilitated Greece into the Eurozone family with the end of its bailout programme. Along with Spain, he was the first to agree to accept the return of refugees now in Germany for registration in Greece as the country of first entry. Refugees seeking asylum had in recent years entered Greece through the Greek Aegean Islands in their thousands, placing enormous strains on local and regional governments coping with years of austerity following a series of draconian EU-IMF financial bailouts.

Summit leaders had further agreed to explore the idea of creating "offshore platforms" but in reality, these would be offshore "camps". This was with the aim of separating economic migrants (to be returned home) from

---

[49]The Human Rights Watch Report 2019.

[50]The suspension of sea patrols as part of operation Sophia in central Mediterranean waters remained in place until 30 September 2019, though air patrols were stepped up. The mission continued training the Libyan coastguard—part of a controversial strategy that critics say led to people being trapped in Libyan detention centres, where they suffer horrific abuse.

[51]www.theguardian.com, 27 March 2019.

genuine asylum seekers, i.e. those escaping wars and poverty. The success of the plan can only be tested in practice. EU leaders stated they wanted to work with international agencies who may be willing to set up migrant camps in North Africa to process asylum claims. But this would have to be with a clear recognition that international norms of UN and international law were observed for the treatment of refugees—to which all EU member states are signatories. But the successful operation of camps in North Africa has no precedent and could not be equated with the EU's refugee 2016 deal with Turkey, a country relatively able in its ability to control the war against terror and with years of experience in handling the fallout from the Syrian Civil War.

The EU needed to convey a signal that it was now moving towards a firmer and more robust approach to migration. The summit was able to present a united front. Both Spain and Greece—as countries of "first arrival"—entered a trilateral agreement with Germany for the return of refugees to be processed on this basis.

However, it has triggered a long overdue debate on the reform of the now flawed EU asylum rules which—based on first-arrival countries' obligation for processing asylum claims—had put a disproportionate burden on southern states nearest to North Africa and Turkey, namely Italy and Greece. While the current refugee flows are smaller than in 2015/2016, these could increase in the future. The growth of failed states and a population explosion in Africa encourage careful planning not only for Europe but also for all developed democracies. The management of migration will remain as important as Eurozone reform for the stability of the EU in future.

Realpolitik in EU Foreign Relations—Negotiating with Autocratic Regimes in the Middle East

The EU is increasingly open to criticism for embracing close ties with a growing list of autocratic rulers and dysfunctional states such as Libya—the gateway to Europe for refugees and economic migrants. This could be viewed as compromising its promotion of democratic values, human rights and civil liberties. But its global engagement has forced it to take a more realistic approach.

Realpolitik now drives EU policy in its international relations. There is a growing acceptance by EU leaders that pragmatism is necessary to accomplish its pressing agenda particularly on migration—as well as on security and international terrorism. In doing so, it meets the agenda of its populist critics in Italy, Central Europe and "old Europe".[52]

The bloc needs a "reality check" and to understand that in an "insecure, multipolar world, 'power' is not a dirty word", stated Mark Rutte, Prime Minister of the Netherlands. "Sometimes you have to dance with whoever's on the dance floor", Mr. Rutte told an audience in Zurich this month—said, no doubt, with his own domestic audience in mind. "We don't always have a choice".[53] Concrete expression of this view is gaining acceptance. In the case of Turkey, it is paramount that the EU avoids any further souring of relations. Too much is at stake. Its agreement with the EU on immigrants is only one dimension and reason for limiting tensions. Turkey is an important trading partner,[54] a member of NATO and a vital ally in containing the Islamic State terror threat now ready to break out in Europe after its final defeat in Syria and Iraq. For its part, Turkey has justified in its criticism with the failure of the EU to honour its agreement in liberalizing visa requirements for Turks wishing to travel to Europe.

> "The EU is trying to find a more realistic foreign policy than it had in the past," says Mr Pierre Vimont, a former first secretary- general of the EU's diplomatic service (2010-2015) now a senior fellow at the Carnegie Europe think-tank. "What is somewhat difficult for the Europeans is to admit it and recognise it."[55]

---

[52]"Old Europe" a term first used in January 2003 by the then US Secretary of defence Donald Rumsfeld in reference to European Countries before the fall of Communism.

[53]www.ft.com, 23 February 2019.

[54]4 largest trading partner of the EU linked by a Customs Union Agreement which came into force 31 December 1995.

[55]*Financial Times*, 24 February 2019.

EU—Dialogue with the Arab League Summit 2019

An EU–Arab summit was held on 24–25 February 2019 in the Egyptian resort of Sharm El Sheikh. This was attended by Angela Merkel the German Chancellor, PM Giuseppe Conte, Italy, and PM Theresa May. The summit gave a platform for addressing migration issues. For the Egyptian host; President Abdel Fattah el-Sisi, the priorities were for joint action in dealing with terrorism—as well as Migration issues. He stated that:

> "Cooperation is necessary between the two regions to secure safe and legal migration in a way that will fulfill several joint interests," he said. "This should go hand in hand with combating human trafficking as part combating cross-border organized crime."

While fighting international terrorism is a prime objective of the EU, Donald Tusk, President of the EU Council in *his* opening address, focused attention on cooperation over migration saying:

> Finally, on migration. I want to acknowledge and salute all those here who have shouldered the burden of population displacement, helped refugees and acted early to tackle people smuggling. We must work together – countries of origin, transit and destination. In order to break the business model of smugglers and traffickers who lure people into dangerous journeys and feed modern-day slavery. To address the root causes of migration and displacement. To stop irregular migration, and facilitate returns, readmission and reintegration. And also to ensure the protection of refugees and their rights, in line with international law.[56]

For the EU Commission, it is increasingly important to develop a firmer and more robust approach to migration policy—as a necessary step in defusing tensions with those anti-immigration EU member states. Populist parties continue to rely on anti-immigration as their mantra and 'raison d'etre for electorate support. But a pro-immigration argument will continue to be promoted while there is no reversal of the demographic decline in countries like Italy and Germany. In Hungary and Poland, the

[56]Council of the EU 133/19, 24 February 2019.

right-wing autocratic governments are endorsing pro-natalist/birth policies offering financial inducements for women to have more than two children to increase birth rates. Increasingly, immigration is seen by populists like Viktor Orban as a drastic remedy. Subsidized child care and nurseries in Norway and Sweden are now given as models to be encouraged elsewhere in the EU—advanced as a key argument for greater intra-European worker mobility. Germany, for example, would not have to boost its labour force from outside Europe when so many EU citizens are unemployed in Southern Europe. This is equally true for the UK where non-EU migration is at its highest since 2004 owing to the decline in arrivals from the EU.[57]

[57]https://www.ons.gov.uk, February 2019.

4
Populism

Defining Populism and its characteristics; populism in the European Union. The rise of Alternative Politics; "Identity Politics" on both Left and Right; The Brexit effect; the effect of 'America first' policies; and Europe's democratic opposition in the fight back.

Populism and the Redrawing of the Political Map of Europe

Right-Wing Populism

Generally speaking, the rise of populism has seen a resurgence of the hard right or far right—as in the case of the UKIP party in Britain. Populism has also eaten into support for traditional centre-right parties like the UK Conservative party, which has lost heavily to the newly formed Brexit party in the polls—falling to as low as 12% against the Brexit Party at around 30% in the polls for the European election on the 23 May.

J. Theodore, *Survival of the European (Dis) Union*,
https://doi.org/10.1007/978-3-030-31214-5_4

In both Germany and Italy, the centre-left socialist parties have been the biggest losers in what is becoming a much fragmented political system.

In northern Europe, successful populists are mainly radical rightwing movements and parties. Parties such as the Finn's Party, the Danish People's Party and the Sweden Democrats all showcase a tough nationalistic stance focusing on opposition to further immigration. Left-wing populism is much less widespread in this part of Europe—likely because the rich economies and comparatively very generous welfare systems of the Nordic countries make a socialist or radical left-wing populist movement less attractive. Left-wing populism has found its strongest base with Podemos in Spain and Syriza, the governing party in Greece, with a predominantly anti-austerity message.

Two important triggers for a drift towards populism in Europe were the fallout from the 2008 global financial crisis, an event which produced nearly a decade of austerity, coupled with unforeseen (and unplanned) mass migration into the EU following the civil war in Syria. The blame game for the 2008 financial crisis meant that established "mainstream" political parties—as part of the established elite—were heavily exposed to criticism for the failure of their economies to ride the storm without punishing consequences for the poor and middle classes. This, coupled with the gross miss-management of the 2014–2016 European refugee crisis, provided populist parties further ammunition to expose incompetence on the part of governing elites in leaving the EU Schengen borders open to the flow of desperate refugees and economic immigrants, and not managing or ameliorating widespread unhappy feeling towards this.

It was therefore no surprise to see the collapse of mainstream parties in both Greece and Italy (and losing ground in others against the rising tide of populism).[1] These are both countries—on the Mediterranean littoral—most hit by austerity (apart from Spain), both entry points for the mass migration of refugees with corruption at all levels of government. Again, many ordinary citizens take the view that ordinary, good and righteous people have been betrayed, neglected or exploited by a corrupt elite. If they decide to cast their vote for populism, it is for a socio-economic populism

[1]Although the Centre Right party (pro-European party) won Greece's General Election on 7 July 2019.

which claims that the true people of the nation are the honest, hard-working (and, implicitly, native) members of the working class—grounded as a contrast to the forces of big business, capital owners and related actors who are perceived and portrayed as propping up an international capitalist system and a wealthy global elite.[2]

Many of the principal grievances today embrace a broad spectrum of EU voters, with the more traditional being class resentment and threatened identities. In Hungary,[3] Poland and the Baltic states, there is the added fear of demographic decline—a decline in which Italy and Germany are statistically in a similar position. Freedom of movement—the flagship of the single market's four principle freedoms for EU citizens—has encouraged the movement of workers seeking higher paid jobs from Bulgaria, Romania and the Baltic states where there are shortages of skilled workers and an ageing population. Each of these grievances (if not the solutions) has a legitimate basis, and all need to be addressed for the more extreme populist tendencies to be contained.

Contrary to popular belief, none of these complaints is strictly economic. In Poland, incomes have been rising and inequality has been falling for 25 years. Yet, in somewhat ironic contrast to this data, ordinary people have become increasingly suspicious of elites feeding themselves at the proverbial trough, while the vast majority allegedly struggle "to make ends meet".[4]

Radoslaw Sikorski, formerly Minister of Foreign Affairs in Donald Tusk's Civic Platform Administration 2007–2014 and a widely cited author and journalist, observes that his country, as with others in Europe, has witnessed an increase in voters populist sentiment and comments. As he says, "Part of the problem is that expectations have outrun reality. When expectations go unmet, people begin to suspect that the social compact itself is unfair. It is this sense of unfairness, far more than income levels, that has fueled support for populist movements. After all, one can earn much more than the Polish minimum wage and still resent the fact that

[2]https://institute.global/insight/renewing-centre/populists-power-around-world.

[3]http://hungarianspectrum.org/2018/06/22/leaving-in-hordes-emigration-from-hungary/.

[4]https://www.livemint.com/Opinion/…/Radosaw-Sikorski--Stealing-the-populists-clothe….

the global rich are squirreling away trillions of dollars in tax havens, or that transnational companies routinely shirk their tax obligations".[5]

In the UK, Brexiteers continue to defend the 2016 referendum leave result as the "will of the people", ignoring the fact that 48.1% voted to remain (with British expatriates losing a Supreme Court bid to vote if living outside the UK for more than 15 years).[6] Anti-establishment populism was the form most prevalent, but cultural populism—associated with national identity—is now the commonest form (of populism) across the globe.

But what this tells you is that populism and nativism are much more complicated phenomena than is often portrayed. In the case of Poland, for instance, these (populism and nativism) are without a doubt rooted in an assertion of Catholicism and Catholic values of the family—as it is in Bavaria with the Christian Social Union (CSU) against the perceived threat of Islam. This is also true for the rise of the Alternative for Germany (AFD) party in Germany and also in Viktor Orban's movement in Hungary. Some of this undoubtedly relates to immigration and some is about Europe's apparently "existential fight" against radical Islam.

Populism in the USA

Trump's America can be identified as part of an anti-establishment revolt,[7] but incorporating a powerful cultural dimension based on a stark appeal to nativism, and the "true" natives of the nation-state as opposed to outsiders such as immigrants and political elites. Trump won the 2016 presidential election—on the back of an "America first" campaign. His electioneering was highly critical of the Washington elites and the liberal establishment prompting him to pledge, if elected, "to drain the (Washington) Swamp". This is hardly a concrete pledge in his manifesto—Trump seeks to keep reminding voters of his apparent outsider status voters when, in reality, his "oligarchical" administration is bristling with billionaires and his close

[5]Ibid.

[6]https://www.bbc.co.uk/news/uk-36370522.

[7]**Anti-establishment populism**: although all forms of populism rail against political elites, anti-establishment populism distinguishes itself by focusing on establishment elites as the primary enemy of the people and does not sow as many intra-society divisions.

family are steering everything from state business to foreign policy in the Middle East. (This is discussed further in Chapters 1 and 7.)

Trump's speeches, policy initiatives and actions to portray immigrants as criminals and "the enemy of the people", together with his ongoing battles with Congress to fund a wall on the Mexican border also reflect the desired actions of Viktor Orban in Hungary, who *has* aped this in erecting a boundary steel fence wall on Hungary's southern border.

Donald Trump's power base is the dispossessed white working classes in de-industrialized cities on the Eastern Seaboard of the USA and forgotten derelict coal mining townships devastated by the outsourcing of production and manufacturing to the Far East since the 1990s. Many of these people can fit into a class of socio-economic populist group as described in a (7 November) 2018 report by the Institute for Global Change.[8]

This report comprehensively defines populism and identifies its global predominance by cataloguing a global database: "Populists in Power: 1990–2018".[9] Here we are more concerned with its impact on the EU and on the EU Parliamentary elections 23–25 May 2019.

Populism as defined in this manner contains two primary claims:

- A country's "true people" are locked into conflict with outsiders, including establishment elites.
- Nothing should constrain the will of the true people.

This report characterizes three main types of populism, distinguished by how populist leaders frame the conflict between the "true people" and outsiders:

- **Cultural populism** claims that the true people are the native members of the nation-state: in contrast to "outsiders", a broad bracket that can include immigrants, criminals, ethnic and religious minorities, and cosmopolitan elites. Cultural populism tends to emphasize religious traditionalism, law and order, sovereignty, and the painting migrants as enemies or "Others". It is typically found on the right.

[8] https://institute.global/insight/renewing-centre/populists-power-around-world.

[9] Ibid.

- **Socio-economic populism** claims that the true people are honest, hard-working members of the working class: the "outsiders" can include big business, capital owners and actors perceived as propping up an international capitalist system. It encompasses the left especially, but is also found on the right.
- **Anti-establishment populism** paints the true people as hard-working victims of a state run by special interests and political elites. Although all forms of populism rail against political elites, anti-establishment populism distinguishes itself by focusing on establishment elites as the primary enemy of the people and does not sow as many intra-society divisions. It can embrace both left and right.[10]

In the tense relations with the EU Commission over imposed immigration quotas, Hungary and Poland have made clear their opposition by emphasizing their belief in ethnicity which, in the populist sense, equates with nativism, an ideology "which holds that states should be inhabited exclusively by members of the native group ('the nation') and argues that non-native elements (persons and ideas) are fundamentally threatening to the nation-state", in the words of Political Scientist Cas Mudde.[11] It is easy to see why populism and nativism are so often intertwined or even perceived as two sides of the same coin: in Europe, most populist parties (74 out of 102) are nativist as well as populist.[12]

In a leading work on this subject entitled "*What is Populism*", Professor Jan-Werner Müller, a Princeton University Political Scientist argues that the central theme of populism is a rejection of pluralism. He goes on to define the main characteristics of populism and the deeper causes of its current electoral success. Like many other commentators, he links it to a form of "identity politics". What the voters backing Matteo Salvini's League, Marine Le Pen's National Rally or Nigel Farage's Brexit Party have in common is a degree of anger unprecedented in the post-war era.

[10]Populists in Power Around the World | Institute for Global .... https://institute.global/insight/renewing-centre/populists-power-around-world.

[11]Cas Mudde. (2010). "The Populist Radical Right: A Pathological Normalcy", *West European Politics* 33, no. 6, p. 1173.

[12]Eiermann, Mounk, and Gultchin, European Populism.

Populists will always claim that they and they alone represent the people and their true interests. This is the message conveyed in many speeches given by strongmen politicians such as President Recep Tayyip Erdogan of Turkey, who for example claimed in a party Congress that, "We are the people who are you" disregarding the fact his party only secured 52% in the 2014 general election.[13]

Viktor Orban in Hungary fastens on to a form of identity politics with his persistent attack on immigration—and an objection to EU imposed quotas. His appeal to voters is an assault on pluralism, encouraging polarization and treating political opponents as "enemies of the people". These political tactics have given his Fidesz party continuing success at the polls. But as with the Law and Justice Party (PiS) in Poland, led by Jaroslaw Kaczynski, he stays in power by dismantling the levers of state control over the executive in contravention of the doctrine of the "separation of powers"—a fundamental concept of democratic government. Both leaders have been systematically eroding the powers of the courts and especially politicizing the independence of their Supreme Courts in fundamental breach of the *rule of law* and adherence to EU Law obligations. This is discussed further in Chapter 6 on illiberal democracies.

The Brexit Effect—And Its Effect on the EU and Eurosceptic Movements

The long-term impact of Brexit on the European Union is still to be assessed. In the short term, there is concern in Brussels within the EU27 that exit negotiations have stalled because of the UK government's inability to get approval for the EU–UK Withdrawal Agreement.[14] Theresa May has failed on 3 occasions to obtain majority support in the Westminster Parliament. This puts the whole of the "divorce" procedure in a state of limbo holding back negotiations discussions—especially during a so-called transitional period for the UK's future relationship. Technically Britain will still remain part of the EU and to the chagrin of Brexiteers subject to EU

[13] politicalcritique.org/file/2015/09/A-Heart-for-Europe-May-2016-FINAL.pdf.

[14] The Withdrawal Agreement has treaty status and was put into legal effect under section 13(1) of the European Union (Withdrawal) Act 2018.

law. It will also remain under the jurisdiction of the European Court of Justice until the end of the "Transitional Period"—unless it crashes out with "no deal". The outcome of post-Brexit future trade negotiations if or when they eventually start will determine the future relationship with the EU.[15] The EU has agreed to a new deadline of October 31 when Brexit will take place with or without a deal. Leaving the EU without deal is universally accepted as most damaging for the British economy. But as Anna Mikhailova, a political correspondent (Daily Telegraph), suggests, the economic arguments don't seem to resonate "with hardline Brexiteers in the European Reform Group (ERG) or 'self- confessed Spartans' who chose to reject the available Brexit option even if it meant risking losing it altogether".[16]

The fact that Britain's political crisis is particularly acute poses a dilemma for the remaining politically mainstream EU leaders. In the EU Council, they have granted Theresa May a further delay, effectively a lifeline, until 31 October 2019 to seek parliamentary approval for the Withdrawal Agreement to exit the EU. Whether or not that can even happen by October, there are substantial risks attached to this in the meantime, not least of which is the legal obligation for the UK to participate in the European elections. Polls already show that the newly formed Brexit party—led by UKIP's former leader Nigel Farage—will be decimated the Conservatives and Labour as polls have them in a comfortable lead with at least 30% of the vote. In the context of a general election, the Conservatives would be out of office on this result. They may well be thinking that the time has come to cut Britain loose to send a warning to others in the hope of discrediting nationalist and illiberal forces who are preparing to disrupt the EU elections. However, they must factor in the risk that a no-deal Brexit—which is still not off the table—would deepen Europe's economic and political crisis, and therefore, ultimately strengthen left- and right-wing populist forces across the continent.

For EU politicians, this is a worrying development even if seen, as many do, as largely a protest vote for May's government's failure to deliver Brexit

[15]For discussion on Hard and Soft Brexit options, see Chapter 5 in "The European Union and the Eurozone Under Stress" (published Palgrave July 2017) by John Theodore, Jonathan Theodore with Dimitrios Syrrakos.

[16]Interview on 3 June 2019 of Anna Mikhailova Political correspondent of the *Daily Telegraph*.

on 29 March. This is primarily due to the spectre of Nigel Farage leading a strong Eurosceptic party into the new European Parliament alongside fellow travellers such as Viktor Orban's Fidesz party and like-minded allies in Poland and the Czech Republic. As with the other European populists, Orban doesn't want to leave the European Union.[17] There is too much to lose in economic terms from the largess provided in the EU Structural Funds that bankrolls infrastructure in his country. The real problem lies in disruption in conducting EU Parliamentary business after the May elections and the appointment of official positions such as the replacement of EU Commission President after Jean-Claude Junker leaves. Premier Orban and his allies promise disruption on challenging EU migration policy on refugees and economic migrants, championing instead nationalist issues and returning further control back to member states.

Populism has played an important role in the Brexit decision to leave the EU. It may never have happened but for UKIP and its charismatic leader Nigel Farage, preaching a message that reflected the concerns and aspirations of the many voters "the left behind" and most to lose by the economic austerity policies of the Conservative–Liberal Coalition government. Industrial and rural communities in northern England have suffered most from years of neglect but as with other EU governments, and it is easier to blame the bureaucrats in Brussels than domestic politicians in London Budapest Athens and Rome. Added to the fear of losing Conservative voters to UKIP—chiefly on immigration and sovereignty issues—it was the need to assuage the Eurosceptic ideologues who are now perched in the European Research Group (ERG) on the right wing of the Conservative party.

Immigration per se has not been such a deciding factor—rather it has been the continuance of uncontrolled EU immigration. Many political parties accept the need for immigration while objecting to the current levels as being unsustainable. Britain has a strong history of being a more

[17]European parties in the EU 27, sympathetic to the Brexit cause are watching closely the unfolding drama of EU–UK withdrawal negotiations. They are presently holding back on any plans to have their own Brexit-style referendums in favor of reforming or destroying the EU from within. The Sweden Democrats, for example, have abandoned their pledge to renegotiate Sweden's place in the EU and to hold a "Swexit" referendum, saying they will now instead "watch and wait" for the impact of Brexit.

outward looking EU nation focused on international trade. But as an island nation (like Ireland) psychologically, it promotes a sense of being different from the rest of the EU "continental" landmass and is not part of the Schengen area set up in 1997 abolishing border controls between signatory member states.

Although one of the largest non-founding members (the three others of the "big four"—Germany, France and Italy—were all founding signatories of the Rome Treaty in 1957), Britain joined later (with Ireland and Denmark) in 1973. But its membership was always perceived by successive British governments as essentially an economic union, rather than a political one. It was Margaret Thatcher's conservative government in 1992 played a key role in supporting development of the single market leading to the adoption of the Single European Act on 1 January 1993. Britain was therefore instrumental in the modernization of the common market but her enthusiasm was less forthcoming for "closer political integration". Black Wednesday on 16 September 1992, when the UK was forced to withdraw from the European Exchange Rate Mechanism (ERM) was a short-term economic disaster that led to a massive devaluation of the pound, and could be referred to as Britain's "first Brexit".[18]

Anglo-Saxon Euroscepticism

There are fundamental differences in the national psychology that has fuelled Euroscepticism in Britain. There is a certain nostalgia for loss of Empire in certain quarters, coupled with a strong belief that Britain was key to defeating Germany in the Second World War (despite of course the substantial help of the USA, the Commonwealth and the Soviet Union to the overall war effort).

This belief tends to play down the role of European countries, even though their countries were occupied between 1940 and 1945. Britain has and remains ambivalent to the sense of unity held by its European neighbours, who share the same continental landmass and feel a need to preserve peace at all costs.

[18]Treasury documents released under the Freedom of Information act confirmed that the cost of leaving the ERM was up to 4 billion Pounds sterling.

"Brexit is an English rather than a British enterprise" is an observation made by Finton O'Toole the famous Irish author and Irish Times journalist who won the Orwell prize for Journalism for his commentary on the Brexit referendum on 15 June 2017—at a ceremony in University College London. His comments focus on English as a separate identity that has been gaining ground over a "Britishness" which had fundamentally been transformed by devolution in both Northern Ireland and Scotland.

To a large extent, this view is borne out by voting patterns that show that Brexit belongs overwhelmingly to provincial England. With the exception of Birmingham, the nation's great cities—London, Manchester, Liverpool and Newcastle among them—were on the side of Remain. They were outvoted by Leavers in smaller English cities and towns and in rural areas, as well as Wales. Scotland backed Remain by a large margin. Even Northern Ireland voted for continued EU membership. In the case of Wales, the genie of nationalism is now out of the box. Although voting marginally to leave the EU a movement for an independent Wales (only 12% at present) was on the March in Cardiff on 11 May with its leader, Adam Price, of the Nationalist party, Plaid Cymru, stating that Welsh problems could be more easily solved if decisions were taken within the nation, adding that:

> Decades of Westminster neglect have resulted in poverty and under-investment. A third of our children are living in relative poverty and you only have to look at the Brexit chaos to see that Westminster is not fit to govern or represent Wales.[19]

Without the EU there is a belief that the UK can fall back on its role as an open trading nation, one cementing new trading agreements with the USA and Commonwealth countries. This is with the proviso, even among the most ardent Brexiteers, that a comprehensive EU–UK trade agreement is established, given that 43–45% is currently conducted with the EU27. The future relationship has to recognize that in some matters Britain simply cannot go it alone. It may be an island, but its security and

[19]https://www.theguardian.com/uk-news/2019/may/11/thousands-march-in-cardiff-calling-for-welsh-independence.

the fight against terrorism require it to work closely with its European partners. How to leave the EU without leaving Europe will remain an important challenge in the years to come.

The Fight Back Against Populism and Authoritarianism in Eastern Europe

Right-wing populists governments control in Hungary, Poland and Slovakia, although holding in most cases no more than 33–35% of the vote. But there is growing evidence of democratic resistance in these nations. These manifest themselves in widespread street rallies. The same has been seen in London, when in March 2019 an estimated one million (though the numbers may well have been exaggerated by "People's Vote" advocates) took to the streets of London to express their opposition to Brexit and the current negotiations for exiting the EU. Most in interviews expressed support for a second referendum.

The fear many pro-European democrats hold is that the current polarization of European politics will work to the advantage of the populist right, particularly in the European Parliamentary elections (23–25 May 2019). There have been mass demonstrations in Warsaw Poland. In Bratislava, Slovakia's capital, a stunning condemnation of Slovakia's populist governing party was offered when Zuzana Caputova—a 45-year-old lawyer, activist and political newcomer—was elected on 30 March 2019 as the nation's first female President. Riding a wave of popular discontent over widespread corruption, she has vowed to return a sense of decency and decorum to Slovakia's often toxic political climate—in this regard, she refused to make direct personal attacks on her opponents mired in corruption allegations. Her sweeping victory, winning 58.1% of the vote in a runoff election, gave a ray of hope to opposition parties across Central Europe that the tide might be turning against narrow ethnic nationalism and related populist movements that have taken power in recent years.

Ms Caputova's victory came a year after the brutal murder of an investigative journalist Jan Kuciak, who had been conducting investigations of corruption at the top levels of government. The scandal led to the resignation of Robert Fico the Slovak Prime Minister. Kuciak's death will remind the public of the murder of Daphne Anne Caruana Galizia, the Maltese anti-corruption journalist where the authorities have failed to find her killer. Caputova gained her support with her messages of decency and civility that endeared her to voters eager for change. She evoked the spirit of Vaclav Havel, the poet and first President of the post-communist Czech Republic who famously wrote about the "power of the powerless" in the face of authoritarianism, and during the 1989 Velvet revolution his slogan was "truth and love will overcome lies and hatred".

Caputova's political credentials are firmly pro-European expressing social and liberal values in keeping with equality and civic rights. She supports gay marriage and a woman's right to choose an abortion. As a lawyer and activist, she has been a staunch critic of abuses of power and crony capitalism deals between politicians and businessmen. She is a member of "Progressive Slovakia", a new liberal party.

Caputova and her allies in Central European must learn from the tactics of the populist "establishment" in both Poland and Hungary to fight for democratic values. Reaching out to socially conservative elements as the Law and Justice Party (PiS) has greatly helped to broaden their electoral base. PiS has harnessed the support of the church in Poland so winning over traditionalist Catholic networks in a country that is overwhelmingly Catholic (66%) in the fight for democratic rule may serve it well.

For many who protested against this last year, the populism of the governing centre-left party—with its unrelenting attacks on both migrants and the European Union, mirroring that of their neighbours in Hungary—amounts to little more than a smokescreen to hide the wholesale corruption at the very top of government.

Opposition in Poland

In July 2018, there were massive protests in Poland over the arbitrary governmental judicial reforms, in formal breach of the rule of law, and the direct appointment of the judiciary in breach of the doctrine of the "separation of powers". The EU, sharing the protesters concerns, triggered the rule of law procedure discussed in Chapter 6 to put pressure on the Polish government to back down.[20]

With the EU Parliamentary elections in mind, a strong opposition is being built hoping to unite against PiS. The biggest-former party in government between 2007 and 2014 is Poland's centre-right Civic Platform (European People's Party). It has formed a broad "European Coalition" by joining forces with the other opposition parties. This is in order to mount a successful challenge to the ruling ultra-conservative Law and Justice Party (PiS). For the socialist Democratic Left Alliance and the Greens, the only way to defeat the Law and Justice Party in the EU elections in May is to join forces with Civic Platform, the largest opposition party.[21] Grzegorz Schetyna, who leads Civic Platform, will head up the new opposition alliance in the EU elections.

This move has received widespread support from many famous former Polish prime ministers and senior ministers, such as Radek Sikorski, the well-known former Minister of Foreign Affairs. Civic Platform politicians have called on all opposition parties to unite in a grand coalition.

Such a broad coalition would guarantee that a pro-EU alliance could directly and seriously compete with the ruling conservatives. Polls suggest that such an alliance could count on 33.2% of the vote, compared to 33.9% for Law and Justice. Schetyna and his allies have ambitions not only to create the European Coalition of Opposition Forces ahead of the European Parliament elections in May but as he says: "This new democratic alliance, which I lead, is already ahead in the opinion polls and is on its way to defeating PiS – first in May, and then in Poland's general election this autumn".[22]

In Hungary, Momentum, a party of Hungarian liberals, and the new face in the opposition alliance have rallied to overcome differences with other opposition parties to present a common front against Viktor Orban's Eurosceptic right. Its deputy leader Anna Donath is the granddaughter

[20]http://europa.eu/rapid/press-release_IP-19-1957_en.htm.

[21]https://www.euractiv.com/content_providers/euractiv-pl/.

[22]https://www.euractiv.com/section/politics/news/pro-eu-parties-join-forces-in-poland-to-face-off-conservatives/.

of Ferenc Donath, a leading figure in the Hungarian 1956 heroic but ill-fated uprising against the Soviet Union, which will likely give her charismatic appeal across the political spectrum, especially in opposing—with other opposition groups—the deeply unpopular and ill-conceived "slave law" passed by the Fidesz administration, as Ms Donath described it at Momentum's Budapest headquarters:

> "For me, the government's court reforms might be more dangerous – because now it's impossible to say there is rule of law in Hungary – but it's a more complicated issue. The 'slave law' is simple to understand and affects everyone... We have all agreed in early January to make a huge protest across Hungary, to show that this is not a 'Budapest-only' issue", said Ms Donath.
>
> "The unions can really help by combining it with strikes, and with road blockades as well we can kill the life in Hungary, at least for one day. That will send a sign, and it has never happened before" under Mr Orbán, she added.[23]

Momentum still has a fight on its hands. Viktor Orbán, speaking on 10 January in Budapest, called on "anti-migration politicians" to take over Europe's institutions after May's elections, welcoming a new partnership between Poland's rightwing government and Italy's populist interior minister, Matteo Salvini.

"This is a topic that is radically transforming European politics, it's the defining political process in Europe", Orbán said at a rare press conference in Budapest on Thursday. "The party structures, traditionally left or right, are being taken over by a different dimension – those for migration and against immigration".

Orbán has unequivocally stated that Hungary's goal was to gain an anti-immigration majority in the European Parliament followed by the executive European Commission, and, later, the European Council, where national leaders make the most critical decisions in European Union.[24]

---

[23]https://www.irishtimes.com/news/world/europe/new-generation-taps-hungary-s-protest-tradition-to-take-on-orb%C3%A1n-1.3740902.

[24]https://www.theguardian.com/.../viktor-orban-calls-anti-migration-politics-take-over-eu-....

The dissident forces that now challenge the Europe-wide wave of populism confidently rely on steadily gaining ground to defeat right-wing populist parties—parties whose governance offers little more than anti-immigration rhetoric with no cogent policies for economic growth and prosperity. This is not to say populism is over in Central Europe, by any means. But it is in the process of being checked and contained in its tracks.

Joining the chorus of anti-establishment sentiment, Vladimir Putin in an interview with the Financial Times Vladimir Putin said that "the liberal idea" had "outlived its purpose" as the public turned against immigration, open borders and multiculturalism .... He went on to say": "[Liberals] cannot simply dictate anything to anyone just like they have been attempting to do over the recent decades", while acknowledging liberalism has been the dominant Western ideology since the end of the Second World War, his statement reinforced support for all anti-establishment leaders from US President Donald Trump to Hungary's Viktor Orban, Matteo Salvini in Italy and the Brexit insurgency in the UK.[25]

[25]https://www.ft.com/content/2880c762-98c2-11e9-8cfb-30c211dcd229.

5

The EU's Illiberal Democracies

Introduction

The rise of pan-European autocracies – tensions with Hungary and Poland (playing the nationalist card) – rule of law and unintended consequences for the political stability of Europe. Conditionality for future funding on Rule of Law observance.

The Clash with Europe's Illiberal Democracies

Europe's crisis of democracy and the rule of law did not surface in a vacuum. It developed gradually after the Eurozone financial crises from 2010 and was reinforced by the ineffective responses of the EU institutions to these problems.

The recent rise of pan-European autocracies is changing the political map of domestic politics in some EU member states. It is of particular concern for electorates in Hungary and Poland, where autocratic regimes—also branded as "populist" governments—are curtailing the rules-based system which they signed up to when joining the EU bloc in 2004.

J. Theodore, *Survival of the European (Dis) Union*,
https://doi.org/10.1007/978-3-030-31214-5_5

For the European Union, this presents a serious challenge. Anti-establishment parties are mushrooming in most EU states some with autocratic tendencies. The forthcoming European Parliamentary elections will act as a sounding board for how serious this new phenomenon will become and whether the EU project—in its present form—can survive the assault on its liberal values.

Hungary and Poland are accused of institutionalizing their "illiberal" democracies in defiance of fundamental democratic principles enshrined in the EU treaties. Both nations are signatories to the 2004 Accession agreement compliance regulations in the *Acquis Communautaire*. Article 2 Treaty of Lisbon–Treaty on the European Union states:

> The Union is founded on the values of respect for human dignity, freedom, democracy, equality, the rule of law and respect for human rights, including the rights of persons belonging to minorities. These values are common to the Member States in a society in which pluralism, non-discrimination, tolerance, justice, solidarity and equality between women and men prevail.[1]

But the Hungarian Prime Minister, Viktor Orban, for his part, takes immense pride in public speeches (mainly to his home base) *and posing* as the saviour of Hungary and the rest of Europe from the supposed evils of (non-EU) migration from the Muslim countries of the Middle East and Africa. He is quoted as saying "The age of liberal democracy is at an end", to the Hungarian Parliament shortly after Fidesz won a third successive term last year. "It is no longer able to protect people's dignity, provide freedom, guarantee physical security or maintain Christian culture".[2]

As the most outspoken of the Central European leaders, Orban takes pride of place as leading challenger to EU liberal values. With great effect, he has deployed Europe-wide opposition to the mass (non-EU) immigration of nearly a million Syrian and other refugees from war-torn Africa and the Middle East, who were provided with sanctuary in Germany by the Merkel government in 2015/2016.

---

[1]Treaty of Lisbon–Treaty on the European Union CONSOLIDATED VERSION OF THE TREATY ON EUROPEAN UNION.

[2]https://www.theguardian.com/.../viktor-orban-showdown-with-eus-centre-right-looms-fo....

The erection of strong external border fences on Hungary's southern flank with Serbia and Croatia was the first physical manifestation of this policy. Going further, Orban has successfully bolstered his Fidesz party's dominance in the Hungarian Parliament—transforming it into a party that seems increasingly united by its commitment to *nativism*, *authoritarianism* and *populism*—the holy trinity of the radical right. Orban takes great pride in labelling Hungary with the mantra of an "illiberal democracy" ignoring the liberal social principles claiming:

> "The age of liberal democracy is at an end", he said when addressing the Hungarian Parliament shortly after his party, Fidesz, won a third successive electoral victory in 2018. "It is no longer able to protect people's dignity, provide freedom, guarantee physical security or maintain Christian culture" or protect the rest of Europe from the supposed evils of migration from the Middle East and Africa.[3]

Nationalism has been combined with authoritarianism, with the government increasingly cracking down on media and NGOs considered "disloyal" to the nation (i.e. to him and his party, Fidesz). Orbán presents himself as the authentic voice of the Hungarian people who are fighting off a (EU-sponsored) left-wing conspiracy. His crusade doesn't stop there. He is determined to engineer a coalition of "anti-migration politicians" to take over EU institutions. This is despite the fragmentation of those right-wing populist forces in the composition of the new European Parliament post the May elections.

Furthermore, he has galvanized a new partnership between Poland's right-wing government and Italy's populist interior minister, Matteo Salvini. The clear intention of this pact is to disrupt the political status quo and with the aim of gaining an anti-immigration majority in the European Parliament, followed by the executive European Commission; and, later, the European Council, where national leaders make the most critical decisions in European Union.[4]

"This is a topic {immigration} that is radically transforming European politics, it's the defining political process in Europe", Orbán said at a

[3]Guardian.com, 17 March 2017.

[4]https://www.theguardian.com/.../viktor-orban-calls-anti-migration-politics-take-over-eu-....

rare press conference in Budapest on Thursday. "The party structures, traditionally left or right, are being taken over by a different dimension – those for migration and those against immigration".[5]

Hungary is part of the Schengen area of 26 European countries (of which 22 are EU members) and is fully aware that it must accept the restrictions governing EU membership. Fidesz, the governing party in Budapest, is attempting to alter the significance of Hungary's "borders". It cannot alter the physical borders imposed on it at the end of the First World War. These were established under the Treaty of Trianon in 1919 (after the Treaty of Versailles). This treaty, still much discussed today in the country, has always been viewed by Hungary as a draconian punishment for siding with Germany and Austria in the First World War—although it is hard to see what choice Hungary had as the junior partner in the Austro-Hungarian Empire. The treaty stripped Hungary—a land-locked country—of much of its former territories, leaving it with less than 93,000 square Kilometres and less than 10 million inhabitants—a number depleted further by many skilled workers emigrating to the west under the mobility accords granted by freedom of movement rules in EU law.

In response to this, the Fidesz government decided to grant substantial tax inducements to Hungarian families to increase native birth rates by having more children, promising no taxation for Hungarian women with four or more children. Further material support was given for families with three or more children to buy a car and increased funding for day care centres and kindergartens. *"In all of Europe there are fewer and fewer children, and the answer of the west to this is migration", said Orbán in his annual state of the nation address on Sunday. "They want as many migrants to enter as there are missing kids, so that the numbers will add up. We Hungarians have a different way of thinking. Instead of just numbers, we want Hungarian children. Migration for us is surrender".*[6]

To kindle a sense of national identity, Orban went further by generously offering all "ethnic Hungarians" citizenship of Hungary, but in accepting

[5]https://www.theguardian.com/world/2019/jan/10/viktor-orban-calls-anti-migration-politics-take-over-eu-matteo-salvini.

[6]https://www.washingtonpost.com/gdpr-consent/?destination=%2fworld%2feurope%2fhungary-is-so-desperate-for-kids-mothers-of-four-wont-pay-income-tax%2f2019%2f02%2f11%2f04701764-2e01-11e9-ac6c-14eea99d5e24_story.html%3f&utm_term=.e2b6a9642a6f.

this offer he (Orban) would still wish them to remain in their former area of pre-Trianon treaty Hungary—which includes a slice of Slovakia, western Romania, known as Transylvania, and part of Ukraine's borderlands with Hungary. This is all gauged to feed the "nationalist" fervour fostering a greater nostalgic sense of (national) identity stimulating a closer-knit Hungarian "diaspora". But this brand of nativism goes side by side with an increasingly authoritarian regime that continues to clamp down on the media, muzzling civic society and the operations of NGOs, and censoring free speech including freedom of the press. It also involves finding scapegoats, particularly in the persona of George Soros, an internationally famous philanthropist of (Jewish) Hungarian origin who has over the years funded countless educational and social causes in the country of his birth, but who is constantly accused of orchestrating a left-wing conspiracy—a charge which has now led to the closure of the Central European University, a flagship beneficiary of the Soros foundation.

What has the EU done to intervene in this threatening series of events? The European Commission has only deployed a piecemeal and scattershot approach so far: several infringement proceedings in fields ranging from the independence of the judiciary to asylum legislation compliance were pursued. However, the Commission was never bold enough to take the next step in the Article 7 procedure or the Rule of Law Framework which proceeds it (which they did in Poland).[7]

The Rule of Law Framework is a mechanism for intensifying dialogue between the EU Commission and a Member State, which aims to restore the rule of law in that "Member State" before more serious legal measures are deployed. When the Hungarian government rapidly changed the Constitution and introduced the compulsory early retirement age of judges, the EU Commission took legal proceedings to the ECJ and the judgement of the court of justice on 6 November 2012 "Commission v Hungary"[8] which held that changes in legislation were contrary to EU law.

Although Hungary subsequently changed the law, it was too late—as the majority of the judges removed did not return to their original posts,

[7]https://spectator.clingendael.org/en/publication/hungarys-systematic-threat-eu-core-values#footnote4_dahhymh.

[8]https://spectator.clingendael.org/en/publication/hungarys-systematic-threat-eu-core-values#footnote7_5nn365o.

partly because their previous positions had already been filled. The Hungarian government has often deployed this tactic, which demonstrates precisely why it is crucial to go beyond basic infringement protocols and proceedings if breaches of EU law with regard to democratic, civil or judicial proceedings persist. At first glance, it looks like Hungary is complying with Court decisions, but on deeper inspection this is only on a surface level—in practice, the desired outcomes for the ruling party are still being achieved.[9]

But resistance to Orban's flagrant contempt for EU values and principles has started to surface. Fidesz has been sanctioned by its allies in the European Parliament. The rightwing European People's Party (EPP), which Orban's Fidesz party belongs to in the European Parliament has decided to suspend—but not expel—Fidesz from its ranks which means that Fidesz party members would not be allowed to attend EPP meetings or nominate party candidates for EPP posts. Two matters would have to be resolved before restoring full membership. Fidesz would have to end its "fake" news campaigns against the EU Commission President and a "clarification" of the "pending legal issues regarding the Central European University" (CEU) a flagship "beacon" of liberal values based in Budapest and funded by the George Soros foundation.[10]

Article 7 Procedure

On 12 September 2018, the European Parliament decided that the state of Hungarian democracy and the rule of law had reached such a worrying level that the EU had to take immediate action. In a historically unprecedented move, Parliament triggered the Article 7 EU Treaty procedure—one that could lead to significant sanctions for the targeted member state, such as Hungary losing its say in new EU laws and legislation.

[9] Member of European Parliament (MEP) Judith Sargentini was assigned the task of drafting this report. The report includes a long list of issues that—taken together—constitute a clear risk of a serious breach of the shared values of the EU by Hungary. In September 2018, Parliament adopted the report with the required two-thirds majority and concluded that protection of EU values must immediately be guaranteed through the commencement of the Article 7 procedure.

[10] The Central European University (CEU) has been forced to relocate its main campus from Budapest to Vienna.

The fact that a member state could be subject to such scrutiny and sanction, with a potential forfeit of its key membership rights, is an extremely serious matter for the political and democratic position of the EU and its institutions.[11] But how did things get to this point? And what does the future hold for the EU and its self-declared values?

To nationalists in Europe Orbán is a champion opposing the established Liberal democratic order. The very embodiment of a *nativist* leader, he is willing to stand up in defence of what he calls "Christian Europe". He has found admirers in the former UKIP leader Nigel Farage, now leader of the UK Brexit Party, as well as Italy's Matteo Salvini Minister of the Interior of the Italian Coalition government.

To Liberals in Europe (and Hungary), Orban is seen as a serial autocrat in the mould of a proto-Russian oligarch. He stands accused of chipping away the keystones of the check-and-balances for the maintenance of democratic institutions, press freedom, independence of the judiciary and the rule of law. He is noted for presiding over a highly corrupt regime, where nepotism is rife, and where opposition is muted by aggressive tactics designed to prevent scrutiny of the corruption that is taking place—and where a hostile environment is created that represents an illiberal, eroding democracy rather than that of healthy and functioning civil society.

Most recently, in December 2018, the Hungarian Parliament adopted new laws that allows for much longer work overtime (often deemed the "slave law" by its many critics) and the establishment of new administrative courts that have jurisdiction on matters like elections, corruption and the right to demonstrate—all extremely sensitive from a political, civil and democratic point of view. Following these latest measures by the government, thousands of Hungarians have been in open defiance on the streets of Budapest for weeks.

[11] Member of European Parliament (MEP) Judith Sargentini was assigned the task of drafting this report. The report includes a long list of issues that—taken together—constitute a clear risk of a serious breach of the shared values of the EU by Hungary. In September 2018, Parliament adopted the report with the required two-thirds majority and concluded that protection of EU values must immediately be guaranteed through the commencement of the Article 7 procedure.

On Hungarian Independence Day, Friday 15 March 2019, Viktor Orban used the occasion to praise Poland's historical links and friendship with Hungary in the presence of the Polish Premier Mateusz Morawiecki, declaring that (we) Central European illiberals will stick together. "We are preparing for a central European renaissance of overwhelming power", said Orbán on Friday. "When Poland is attacked from Brussels, the attack is against the whole of central Europe, and against us Hungarians. To empire builders who seek to cast their shadow over central Europe, we have this to say: they will always need to reckon with the strong bonds between Poland and Hungary".[12]

Common to many populist leaders is the channels and tools by they address and expand their voter base. For Viktor Orban, speeches play a big part. But their real success is in the ability to weaponize the modern technology of political communication. The onset of the digital age has radically changed this, by easing the way politicians can connect more directly with voters (on a daily basis) through the various social networks such as Facebook and Twitter. The effective use of these networks has been critical in, for example, the campaign for the US presidential election of Donald Trump in 2016 and in both the UKIP Brexit Referendum and Italian 2018 general election campaigns.

The power of social media provides a conduit for massive political disinformation campaigns, as was for example alleged in the recent Brazilian presidential campaign of Jair Bolsonaro conducted on WhatsApp.[13] Social media can also benefit pro-democracy crusades but generally it is populists, autocrats and far-right parties that benefit the most. Controlling the spread of fake news on social media is more difficult and even if corrections are made, it is often too late to limit any political fallout to alter social divisions that may have been inflamed by them. With the fallout from the Cambridge Analytica[14] scandal in the UK, there is a renewed effort by the EU to monitor data protection rules clearly set out in its Strategic

[12] https://www.theguardian.com/.../viktor-orban-showdown-with-eus-centre-right-looms-fo....

[13] The popular messaging app owned by Facebook.

[14] The 2018 case revealed that personal data of millions of people's Facebook profiles had been "harvested" without their consent for political purposes.

Agenda 2019–2024.[15] Interviewed on Channel 4 on 8 May 2019, Elizabeth Denham, the Information Commissioner has warned parties on their obligations in law—relating to manipulation of voters in the use of social media such as Facebook.

Poland's March Towards Illiberalism and Autocratic Rule

Thirty years ago, Poles overcame their internal political divisions in the Solidarity movement—a trade-union led political movement for freedom which overthrew the communism system that was yoked to the Soviet Union. Solidarity became the beacon of opposition powering the liberal forces that freed Eastern Europe from its vassalage to the Soviet state.

For the past 26 years, the Polish economy has been booming: successfully weathering the global financial crash of 2008 with growth rates far in excess of those in its Eurozone neighbours. The economy (the 8th largest in the EU) has had the benefit of near full employment—partly due to emigration by many Poles to work in the UK and other EU destinations permitted under EU freedom of movement mobility rules.

Civic Platform (a centrist Liberal–Conservative party) led by Donald Tusk[16] was in power for 8 years between 2007 and 2015 before it was ousted by the Law and Justice Party (PiS). When the latter took over in 2015, it set about stripping away the nuts and bolts of the Polish constitution relating to the rule of law and the "Separation of Powers".[17] These actions included a systematic erosion of the independence of the judiciary by the blatant attempt to politicize the appointment of the judges. This gave PiS the governing party political control of the judiciary.

[15] EU Strategic Agenda for 2019–2024—Consilium.europa.eu.

[16] Donald Tusk was appointed President of the EU Council in 2014.

[17] "The Separation of powers" separates the legislature, executive and judicial functions of government.

Brussels Fights Back

The European Commission—the EU's key executive body—referred the matter to the Luxembourg-based European Court of Justice (ECJ), which in October 2018 ordered Poland to "immediately suspend" the application of its new law and to reinstate those judges who had been forced to retire early. The Polish government had argued that the legal reforms—which activated mass street protests—were needed to make the Supreme Court more efficient and remove judges appointed during the communist era. The PiS subsequently conceded that it was reinstating the judges because it respected the rulings of the EU's top court. "We are fulfilling our obligations", Justice Minister Zbigniew Ziobro told MPs.[18]

The head of the PiS, Jaroslaw Kaczynski, said at the time the government would comply with the decision. "We are members of the European Union and we will abide by European Union law",[19] was offered as an adroit statement on his part, noting that daily penalties would now be avoided for non-compliance with the ECJ's ruling. But recognition for the change of heart goes to Chief Justice Malgorzata Gersdorf, head of Poland's Supreme Court (with her retired colleagues), who had refused to step down at 65 years of age citing the government's action to reduce the retirement age as a "purge" on the judiciary.

The government declared it wished to resolve its disputes with the European Commission relating to the changes to Poland's courts since it came to power. This was part of a government rethink in seeking ways to reduce tensions with Brussels by making concessions. Krzysztof Szczerski, chief of staff to the Polish President, signalled Poland's pro-EU credentials—citing that 80% of Poles support the European family and acceptance of single market principles, the four fundamental freedoms at the heart of the EU and the single market.

The PiS government had already appointed the majority of judges to the Constitutional Tribunal, which is empowered to veto legislation, and supervise/control the body that nominates all judges in Poland. The Polish justice minister—who also serves as the prosecutor general—also now has

---

[18] https://www.bbc.co.uk/news/world-europe-46296859.

[19] https://www.bbc.co.uk/news/world-europe-46296859.

the power to appoint and dismiss the deputies and those in charge of the lower courts.

The ruling Law and Justice Party (PiS) in Warsaw, holding only 37.6% of the electoral vote, inherited and continued to preside over a buoyant economy, helped by generous EU subsidies. It has been largely sheltered from the Eurozone crisis. But with reduced funding on the horizon, it is anxious not to lose its share in the new round as this could jeopardize the completion of vital infrastructure projects that prop up its electoral base.

Accusations by members of the European Parliament of creeping authoritarianism by the PiS administration are vehemently denied. The ruling party makes the spurious argument that judicial reforms were necessary to eradicate the legacy of the former communist regime. Critics in Brussels and in Poland's opposition parties disagree with this analysis.

Brussels anticipates this tactic and is ready to deploy a stronger financial deterrent. Poland is keenly aware that adherence to the rule of law may well be made conditional for getting its share of funds in the next EU budget round 2021–2028.[20] Poland is currently the largest beneficiary of European Regional Development Funds. But the bonanza of EU subsidy to the country cannot last. With the UK exiting, the EU in 2019 allocations will be reduced. States such as Austria, Denmark and the Netherlands who are net donors are seeking to put budgets under tighter scrutiny.

The ruling Law and Justice Party (PiS) in Warsaw, holding a mere 37.6% of the electoral vote, has presided over a buoyant economy, helped by generous EU subsidies, has been largely sheltered from the Eurozone crisis. But with reduced funding on the horizon, it is anxious not to lose its share in the new round as this could threaten the country's ongoing economic prosperity. The EU Commission is putting forward policy statements arguing that the allocation of new project funds will depend on states adhering to the rule and principles of EU law—as well as their own laws—and the maintenance of an independent judiciary. This is causing alarm in Poland as the biggest beneficiary (as a proportion of GDP) of EU Structural Funds—funds forecast to be in receipt of billions of euros in the next multi-annual round. Poland received €10.6 bn from the EU in

[20] Which Poland ascribed to as part of the acquis communautaire when joining in 2004.

2016, equivalent to 2.6% of its gross national income, which has supported numerous public projects—especially transport infrastructure.

Poland's Minister of EU affairs, Mr. Konrad Szymanski, recently expressed his concern on 19 February 2018 that these latest tactics in a statement he made in Brussels that: "I see enormous problems related to the implementation of that political concept, because it could lead to limitation of the member states' rights guarded by the [EU] treaty".

Loss of Revenue

With the impending loss of Britain's financial contribution to the EU multi-annual budget, Brussels is seeking ways of making up the shortfall calculated at €13 bn. At the same time, there is strong resistance to any increases in EU budgetary contributions, particularly, from the smaller net contributors, namely Denmark, the Netherlands, Sweden and Austria. The largest net contributor, Germany, understandably, is seeking to link payments to adherence of EU fundamental principles—to which all members are signatories.

Poland and Hungary are already at loggerheads with Brussels over their continued refusal to accept refugee quotas imposed by the EU in addition to the undemocratic "illiberal" policies discussed above.

Poland's Importance to the EU After Brexit

Balanced against these political strains with its EU partners, Poland is recognized as vitally important for military and security purposes. It is a critical buffer protecting Europe's eastern flank against Russia, and on its northern border via the Russian exclave, Kaliningrad. With the departure of the UK in March 2019, it will emerge as the EU's fifth-largest member, both geographically and economically. It shares a border with Ukraine in the south-east and with Belarus to the east, an autocratic nation which is financially dependent on Russia but increasingly looking to strengthen its economic ties with the EU. Unlike Prime Minister Viktor Orban of Hungary, Poland has frosty relations with Russia and is keen to develop closer links with the UK post-Brexit, particularly on military and security matters. Like the UK, it has been a fierce critic of Russia over its annexation of Crimea and its activities in the east of Ukraine. It is busy upgrading its armed forces and purchasing military hardware and actively supports NATO's forward positioning of troops, on its territory as well as in Estonia—policies which serve the interest both Europe and the USA.

The outlook for the EU may appear uncertain but there are the stirring grassroots of a resistance to authoritarian rule especially in Poland. In electoral terms, the opposition to the nationalist regime made some critical gains in September 2018, taking almost all of the larger cities—a vote that also underscored how divided the country is along social and geographic grounds.[21] As a result, the ruling Law and Justice Party may struggle to sustain a majority in future national elections.[22] If so, this would be a momentous shift for the EU and the challenge of populism and nationalism—not least because Poland is the sixth-largest EU nation.[23]

In the new EU Parliament, the right-wing populist forces representing Central and Eastern Europe will focus their agenda on the restoration of powers to their national legislatures. The success of this strategy will be determined in the next EU Parliamentary session and whether they galvanize support from other Eurosceptic groups to further this end. More productive would be to work with the EU institutions in preventing the continued depopulation of their regions caused by lack of investment, low pay and unemployment. The challenge for future stable relations between "old" and "new Europe" is in identifying the importance of investment as a *quid pro quo* for the loss of their high-skilled workforce trained at their expense but now working in the west.

[21] https://www.politico.eu/article/local-elections-deal-a-blow-to-polands-ruling-pis/.

[22] Poland is to hold Parliamentary Elections on 13 October 2019.

[23] https://www.theguardian.com/commentisfree/2018/nov/22/europe-populist-democratic-resistance.

6

The EU, China and Their Changing Relations

Economic relations—how important are they? Reciprocity of market access; The Belt and Road Initiative Europe (OBOR) Strategic concerns; Human rights; Security Issues; Huawei and 5G; Effect of US–China trade tariff wars; Approach to new deals.

EU–China—Commercial Relations

The EU is China's largest trading partner—and China is the EU's second largest trading partner after the USA. Most of this trade is in industrial and manufactured goods—goods which are essential lifeblood for the European economy, particularly with regard to consumer trends.

As with the USA, Brussels is keen to ensure that China trades fairly and to respect Intellectual Property rights and obligations under the World Trade Organization (WTO); it joined on the 11 December 2001. While

This chapter is co-authored between John Theodore and Jonathan Theodore

J. Theodore, *Survival of the European (Dis) Union*,
https://doi.org/10.1007/978-3-030-31214-5_6

China has made progress in the probity of its commercial dealings, criticism continues to be directed to the lack of transparency for outside parties and perceived levels of Chinese government intervention. The Strategic Outlook report[1] asserts that "China preserves its domestic markets for its champions, shielding them from competition through selective market opening, licensing and other investment restrictions; [and offers] heavy subsidies to both state-owned and private sector companies…".[2]

The report goes on to say:

> EU operators have to submit to onerous requirements as a precondition to access the Chinese market, such as creating joint ventures with local companies or transfer of key technologies to Chinese counterparts. One of the sectors where the **lack of reciprocal market access** is particularly acute is financial services. While Chinese fintech and online payment companies, credit cards providers, banks and insurers are expanding their presence in the EU, European operators are denied access to the Chinese market.[3]

The EU is trying to underpin its trade with China by linking it to continued progress on the nation's (questionable) human rights record—a process monitored on an ongoing basis between the EU and Chinese government representatives.[4]

Both the EU and China are keen to increase trade relations and continue to grow a viable strategic partnership. This becomes imperative with the current escalating trade tariff wars China now has with the USA. Crucially, how the EU aligns in this conflict will determine its relationship with both. Additionally, any EU perspective must take account of the interests

---

[1] Defined as promoting sectors such as advanced information technology industry, machinery and robotics, aerospace and aeronautic equipment, marine engineering equipment and high tech ships, advanced rail transport equipment, energy-saving vehicles and renewable energy, agricultural machinery and equipment, new materials, biopharma and high-performance medical products. See 中国制造 2025 (Made in China 2025), State Council, May 8, 2015.

[2] European Commission, "EU-China—A Strategic Outlook," March 12, 2009, at https://ec.europa.eu/commission/sites/beta-political/files/communication-eu-china-a-strategic-outlook.pdf.

[3] EU-China Strategic Outlook European Commission report 12 March 2019.

[4] This is all in marked contrast to the EU's relations with Russia. Europe has been dominated by Russia's occupation of the Crimea—for which the EU maintains a policy of economic sanctions—also Russia's part in fuelling the crisis in the Ukraine, and its military sabre rattling alarming the EU 'Visegrad' and Baltic states.

of the bloc—and be mindful of the vested interests of individual member states.[5] So far, the shaping of EU–China relations has been influenced more by the EU heavyweights France and Germany and Britain—with its less protectionist approach in trade matters. EU enlargement has made this process more difficult when having to accommodate the larger EU28 agenda. China has taken advantage of the economic disparities in the Eurozone and courted countries in South and Central Europe anxious to revive their failing economies. Two Eurozone members, Greece (August 2018) and Portugal (January 2019) have signed as members of the Belt and Road Initiative Europe (OBOR). Since the acquisition of Piraeus port near Athens by the Chinese Ocean Shipping Group Company (COSCO) company in August 2016, Greece has become a major stopover along the new Silk Roads; however, Athens had still not formally joined the BRI. However, in August 2018, Greek and Chinese foreign ministers Nikos Kotzias and Wang Yi signed a memorandum of understanding regarding cooperation within the framework of the "Belt and Road Initiative" during a meeting in Beijing.

This was followed by Italy—the third largest Eurozone economy—signing a memorandum of understanding (MOU) with China on the 23 March 2019.[6]

The 2016 EU Strategy on China remains the cornerstone of EU commitment, providing the basis for delivering a further policy shift towards "a more realistic, assertive, and multi-faceted approach".[7] Both sides are committed to "a comprehensive strategic partnership", as conveyed in the EU-China 2020 Strategic Agenda for Cooperation.[8] This ensures that relations with this strategic partner are set on a fair, balanced and mutually beneficial course.[9] The strategy looks to maintain multilateralism and

[5] Belt and Road Initiative (BRI) or One Belt One Road (OBOR), the brainchild of Chinese President Xi Jinping part of an ambitious plan promoting China as a global leader for economic development.

[6] https://ec.europa.eu/commission/sites/beta-political/files/communication-eu-china-a-strategic-outlook.pdf.

[7] https://ec.europa.eu/commission/…/communication-eu-china-a-strategic-outlook.pdf.

[8] https://eeas.europa.eu/delegations/china_en/15398/EU-China%202020%20Strategic%20Agenda%20for%20Cooperation.

[9] Joint Communication to the European Parliament and the Council—'Elements for a new EU strategy on China', JOIN (2016) 30, 22 June 2016, and Council Conclusions on EU Strategy on China of 18 July 2016.

the global order. This is in contrast to the protectionism and "bilateralism" of Trump's "America first" policy. But in pursuing the promotion of common global interests, the EU should insist on balanced and reciprocal conditions governing the economic relationship. The Strategic Outlook prepared by the EU Commission for the European Parliament, Council and European Council on the 12 March 2019 notes the growing status of China as key global player and leading technological power.

Strategic Concerns

Brussels officially recognizes that: "China can no longer be regarded as a developing country.[10] It is a key global actor and leading technological power. Its increasing presence in the world, including in Europe, should be accompanied by greater responsibilities for upholding the rules-based international order, as well as greater reciprocity, non-discrimination, and openness of its system. China's publicly stated reform ambitions should translate into policies or actions commensurate with its role and responsibility."[11]

Since gaining membership of the World Trade Organization (WTO) in 2001 China has never looked back and today ranks as the second largest economy in the world—giving it increasing influence and power to engage in world affairs and quite rightly a commensurate political status to match. How does this accord with EU foreign policy objectives? There is common ground with the EU where China's foreign policy addresses issues of universal concern such as the environment including climate change, the liberalization of trade, international security and the fight against international terrorism.

The EU perceives China's growing power in accordance with its economic strength and ensuing political position in the world order as a full

[10]The China of Deng Xiaoping (China's leader between 1978 and 1989) was linked to the opening up of China to economic reforms under the slogan of "One Country, Two Systems".

[11]https://ec.europa.eu/commission/sites/beta-political/files/communication-eu-china-a-strategic-outlook.pdf.

membership of the UN Security Council and the G20.[12] But individually, in commercial terms, some EU states (as in the case of Italy and Portugal) have been concerned that they have not been able to compete against the flood of cheap consumer goods including textiles, clothing and footwear from China. The economic attitudes of Germany, France and Poland are inclined towards protectionism—but not all to the same degree.

Beijing has also exploited divisions within the EU 28 (EU 27 when UK exits) members. This can be divided into several categories: those who are more trade protectionist (France, Germany, Poland) from other more ideologically "free-traders" (Denmark Netherlands, Sweden and the UK). The UK falls into the latter grouping—and back in 2013, David Cameron, the UK Prime Minister, led a high-level trade mission to China to initiate a multi-billion euro trade deal independent of the EU Commission's ongoing trade negotiations.[13] With the UK now set to exit the EU on the 31 October (at least in theory, and assuming nor further extensions or a revocation of Article 50 by Parliament to avoid a "no-deal" Brexit), its future trading relations with China will take a bilateral route. Any UK-China deal will, however, have to take account of its future relationship with the EU *and* the USA.

Strategic concerns remain that the EU, in dealing with China, has succumbed to an approach of "unconditional engagement". This has been taken as: a policy that gives China access to all the economic benefits of trading with the EU—but, even with nearly four decades of its "New Open Door" policy, China still maintains multiple barriers to entry for outside investors. Overall, Brussels has been receptive to inward investment as long as it doesn't encroach on Europe's most sensitive industries, such as technology, and where intellectual property rights can be appropriately safeguarded. But criticism has hardened since 2016 to Chinese companies (linked to the Chinese state) getting access to strategically important technological industries, prompting Berlin to push for EU protective measures. This protectionist reaction was sparked by a surge of Chinese deals culminating in a €4.5 billion acquisition of the robot maker Kuka, one of

[12] 1 October 2016, the RMB officially received reserve currency status with a 10.92% weighting in the IMFs Special Drawing Rights. The Chinese RMB was finally, included in the IMF's basket of reserve currencies in December 2015.

[13] https://www.ft.com/content/235ff2da-3bbe-11e6-9f2c-36b487ebd80a.

Germany's most innovative companies, by the Chinese appliance maker Midea—with additional cases given below.[14]

In May 2016, the European Parliament voted against giving China Market Economy Status (MES) by the end of 2016, as notionally provided for when it joined the WTO in 2001.[15] Although China still falls under "emerging" market status, it continues to be criticized for its protectionist policies and lack of reciprocity with regard to access to its internal markets.

Chinese Investment in the Eurozone

Chinese investment (FDI) in the EU is important—particularly in the struggling Eurozone economies of the south. At home, its growth and direct investment abroad—in Africa and through the Belt and Road Initiative (BRI)—are reshaping the world economy. Inward investment in Greece is a good case in point. The best example is its investments in the port of Piraeus (67% share by China's state-owned shipping company Cosco) which the cash-strapped Syriza government was previously reluctant to privatize.

The geopolitical implications of Chinese investment in Europe do raise some key concerns. From an economic viewpoint, there are misgivings that Piraeus—one of the most important seaports in the region—would serve as a platform for China to export and distribute its goods even more widely throughout Europe and the Mediterranean region, potentially competing with Europe's own industrial base.[16] The USA is equally concerned by China's influence in those economies of Eastern Europe that have become part of the Europe 16 +BRI states.

This strategy tracks Beijing's "One Belt, One Road" (OBOR) project—a broad, consciously visionary phrase invoking a string of ports, logistics hubs and other trading infrastructure stretching all the way from Southeast Asia to the north of England. It has its roots in the historic Silk Road—the

---

[14]http:// http://digital.olivesoftware.com/Olive/APA/FinancialTimesUK/#panel=document.

[15]www.crs.gov. congressional Research service 10 January 2019 on China's Status as a Nonmarket Economy.

[16]The European Union and the Eurozone Under Stress Palgrave 2017.

greatest economic achievement of the illustrious Han Dynasty, and the key artery of commerce and culture that connected Europe and Asia for two thousand years—and which could rightly claim to be one of the great economic wonders of the world. In a speech in 2013, Chinese President Xi Jinping announced that the Silk Road would be reborn as the Belt and Road Initiative, consciously intended to be the most ambitious infrastructure project the world has ever seen. In the words of President Xi, the ancient Silk Road embodied the essence of "peace and cooperation, openness and inclusiveness, mutual learning and mutual benefit".[17] Rhetoric aside when finished, the new routes will directly or indirectly connect two-thirds of the entire world's population, and a third of its GDP. China, in essence, aims to become, the beating heart of global trade: the bridges, pipelines, and railroads of Belt and Road the great new arteries of global commerce.

The debate as to how much China has truly been exercising a long-term master plan will continue to be argued. But new investment opportunities in Europe date back to the post-2008 financial crisis and consequent Euro-debt crisis of 2010–2011, when China purchased bonds of Eurozone countries and started to invest increasingly heavily in their infrastructure.[18] The extension of the Belt and Road project into Europe has created rifts between some EU member states.

Brussels is already at odds with Italy over its budget deficit plans and is warning the Italian government of the potential consequences of a bilateral deal with China that endorses its participation in the Belt and Road Initiative. Mark Rutte, the Dutch Prime Minister, put it more bluntly when he said that "We should not be naïve"…. "You have to take into account the possibility that China, through these policies, is pursuing some of its national interests. It can present a problem given the content of those agreements." His remarks were echoed by French President Emmanuel Macron, who stated that "It is not a good method to discuss bilateral agreements on the new 'Silk Road'".[19] A bilateral approach by Italy and

[17] https://www.worldbank.org/en/topic/regional-integration/brief/belt-and-road-initiative.

[18] http://euasiaegf.net/chinas-offensive-in-europe-is-there-a-master-plan-in-beijing/.

[19] Euractiv.com, 22 March 2019.

some Eastern European states underscores the ability to preserve a common EU position on future Chinese investment.[20] President Macron has been keen to encourage other member states to "Europeanise" their China policies.

At a joint meeting in June 2019, Macron invited the EU Commission President, Jean-Claude Junker, to join him with China's President Xi Jinping and Chancellor Merkel of Germany to present a united front interlinking intergovernmental institutions with the main EU institutions. Macron is providing a sounding board of caution on how, and in what manner, EU member states engage with China. This is as they are forced to note that its economic rise is based on a system of control that survives from the old Maoist communist regime. Modern-day China is effectively a merchant state run by an Orwellian-like, surveillance-obsessed authoritarian government whose primary claim to legitimacy is that it made China rich. These riches have been created by opening up the Chinese economy to the world and carving out a private sector from the old state industries. But such economic liberalism has only gone part of the way to match the "Western model"—the Chinese government is still characterized by a "state capitalist" economic system shaped by massive state intervention in the economy, and which also enforces an uneven playing field for foreign competitors.

A conscious and open recognition of these realities characterize the avowed new approach to China by the EU and its member states and is now expressed in the European Commission's "strategic outlook" on EU-China relations. The outlook report states that

> The ability of EU and China to engage effectively on human rights will be an important measure of the quality of the bilateral relationship. The EU acknowledges China's progress in economic and social rights. However, in other respects, the human rights situation in China is deteriorating, notably in Xinjiang and regarding civil and political rights, as witnessed by the continuing crackdown on human rights lawyers and defenders. The

[20] Greece joined the "16+1" group of eastern European countries to join the Belt and Road Initiative with China.

human rights of EU and other foreign citizens in China must be protected. The high degree of autonomy enshrined in the Hong Kong Basic Law needs to be respected.

It also acknowledges that:

EU companies often encounter difficulties to gain access to procurement opportunities in the Chinese as well as other foreign markets, in particular in sectors where EU companies are highly competitive (e.g. transport equipment, telecommunications, power generation, medical equipment and construction services). **This protectionist trend is rising.**[21]

Security Issues

From all this, it is still absolutely clear that Chinese foreign investment is expected to grow throughout Europe in the years to come. Historically, fallout of the Financial and Eurozone debt crises, coupled with the substantial fall in the Euro, have helped China as a foreign investor and influence. Some of its leading corporations have created new partnerships within the European Union, working to expand the country's power through finance and infrastructure. As an example of this, Piraeus (Europe's mainland Mass Migration entry point via the Aegean sea) can be identified as a crucial hub of China's objective for its new Silk Road, "One Belt, One Road" connecting Europe to China via sea and land. This has raised key issues of national security in Europe. This also concerns the USA,[22] as some of the Chinese investments in Greece as elsewhere are perceived as part of a geopolitical plan to expand China's broader influence, and not simply strict economic gain.[23]

[21] https://ec.europa.eu/commission/sites/beta-political/files/communication-eu-china-a-strategic-outlook.pdf. Bold has been added to the last line for emphasis.

[22] China-US rivalry in the South China seas.

[23] For Greece, a member of NATO, an investment of such strategic importance does raise issues of dependency national security and sovereignty but one that the Greek government can balance off against the economic benefits it brings to its crisis-ridden economy.

Views, however, do vary on this matter. Peter Mandelson, the former EU Trade Commissioner and Business Secretary in Gordon Brown's Labour administration, has suggested… "It would be commercially and globally suicidal for China if they were to invest on the one hand and then try to mess around with other countries' security", adding "Nobody would trust Chinese investment again, nobody would want to do business with China again."[24] On a separate note, China sees the USA as its ultimate competitor, both economically and politically—*not* Europe, where it views its links more in terms of continued and expanding economic engagement, with geopolitics a relative sideshow so far.

Other EU countries have become beneficiaries of Chinese FDI—including the UK, which negotiated with the French company EDF Energy and Chinese state-backed company CGN to regenerate the British nuclear power industry. Delays by the government of Theresa May in July 2016 in giving the go-ahead to a deal with CGN and EDF to construct the Hinckley nuclear power plant (in Somerset) were viewed in business and political circles as a mistake—although the contract was finally approved.

Peter Mandelson, who had formerly led EU trade delegations to Beijing during his term of office as EU Trade Commissioner in Brussels, believed that: "the UK has no choice but to preserve the China relationship, as after Brexit the UK will be "dependent on China's goodwill."

"Out of the EU, we are probably more dependent on China's goodwill because we need to replace trade lost in Europe" Mandelson stated in a BBC Radio interview soon after the Brexit referendum. "We will want to deepen our economic ties with China post-Brexit. It'll be a major foreign economic-policy priority for the country. I don't think that making any move in the meantime that makes that more difficult—and difficult enough it is going to be—is in Britain's interest."[25]

Mandleson's comments apply equally to Brussels on how it plans to conduct its China relations. This becomes a critical challenge since the breakdown in the US–China relationship manifesting itself in the ongoing tariff wars. The EU (and the UK) are witnessing a radical change in US

---

[24] http://www.politico.eu/article/peter-mandelson-uk-has-no-choice-but-to-preserve-china-relationship/.

[25] http://www.bloomberg.com/news/articles/2016-08-10/mandelson-urges-u-k-nuclear-deal-with-prized-partner-china.

policy towards China. US economic and technological supremacy is under threat but the Trump administration makes no secret of its aim to win this race against China.

Huawei and 5G

Huawei is caught in the midst of the larger US–China trade war. The company is the world's No. 1 telecom supplier and No. 2 phone manufacturer. Yet it is effectively a pariah in several countries, including the USA and UK.

The core issue with Huawei has been concerned about its very close relationship with the Chinese government, and fears that its equipment could be used to spy on other countries and companies. Fears that Huawei may be complicit in Chinese state surveillance are the reason that the USA banned companies from using Huawei networking equipment as far back as 2012. This did not stop Huawei smartphone sales rising rapidly in the USA—or the EU and UK. Added to this is Trump's more belligerently nationalistic trade policy, with an avowed goal to deal with what he perceives, and his administration touts, is China's unfair grip on the global economy, at the apparently expense of US jobs (a point disputed by most mainstream economists[26]).

Ongoing tensions with the company came to a head on 15 May 2019, when the company was added to the US Department of Commerce's Bureau of Industry and Security Entity List, following an executive order from President Donald Trump that effectively banned Huawei from US communications networks.

The blacklisting imposed by Trump represented a body blow to China's most vaunted technology company This was an all-out trade embargo on the company that, in a globalized economic system meant that about 1200 US suppliers of components and intellectual property to Huawei and its 68 affiliates would have to stop business with it—including everyone from Google with their Android phone operating system, to British-born chipmaker ARM Holdings. The embargo is expected to produce a 30

[26]https://www.bbc.co.uk/news/business-47369123.

billion revenue miss for the beleaguered tech giant, on their own estimates alone.[27]

For the Chinese government, Huawei is treated as something akin to a national treasure, a core player in its state capitalist system and global plans for economic expansion. There are also numerous precedents for Chinese surveillance and broad-based information gathering. But Huawei has long denied any wrongdoing and continues to maintain its innocence through the recent charges.

In the words of Ren Zhengfei, the founder of the company, in an interview with the BBC, "The Chinese government has clearly said that it won't ask companies to install backdoors." A "backdoor" is a phrase used to describe a secret software entry point in a computer system that gives access to the person or entity who installed it to the inner workings of that system, and potentially all the data on it.

Ren further iterated that "Our sales revenues are now hundreds of billions of dollars. We are not going to risk the disgust of our country and our customers all over the world because of something like that. We will lose all our business. I'm not going to take that risk."[28] So far at least, a "smoking gun" proving their complicity in Chinese surveillance and data harvesting has not been discovered or revealed.

US Pressure on Both the EU and UK Post-Brexit

At a time when China is the main industrial supplier to Europe, the USA is determined that the globalization of China's technology is contained—and the apex of this issue so far has been the blocking of Huawei supplying of equipment for the West's telecom systems The USA has been pushing allies for months to bar the Chinese company entirely from their 5G networks on national security grounds, warning that its telecoms equipment could be used by Beijing for spying and enhance Chinese state interference across the globe. But the EU and Britain are using high-performance and relatively low-cost Chinese equipment to construct the next generation

[27] https://www.cnbc.com/2019/06/19/huawei-ceo-downplays-companys-expected-30-billion-revenue-miss.htm.

[28] https://www.bbc.co.uk/news/resources/idt-sh/Huawei.

of ultrafast 5G broadband systems. As a consequence, the UK's refusal to embrace a blanket ban on Huawei has become one of the most sensitive issues in the relationship between the UK and the USA. But the UK still looks likely to shut Huawei out of parts of its still-developing 5G networks—a move which is controversial not just on the Chinese side. According to the head of Ericsson's US business, Niklas Heuveldop, the UK's plan to shut Huawei out of parts of the network makes little technical sense and any plan to allow a company such as Huawei to supply equipment to "noncore" parts of 5G networks but not the "core" misunderstands how the network will work. He warned that countries should choose either to allow companies complete access, or none at all.[29]

For the UK, this whole controversy, as a proxy for the US–China trade war in general, poses substantial problems for its relations with both China and the USA. With the latter, it is trying to expand its "special relationship" with an ambitious Free Trade Agreement (FTA) post-Brexit. A bilateral UK-US deal outside the EU will pose challenges, as the US administration has signalled via the words of Trump at a press conference with Theresa May that "nothing is off the table": a suggestion which, if meaningful, could adversely affect *inter alia* the UK agricultural and pharmaceutical sectors, and potentially even state services such as healthcare.[30]

On the Chinese side, a Free Trade Agreement with China is also at risk if the UK government follows Washington line. A £200 million contract for the export of British beef—a huge boost to the farming sector—could be at risk. Mr Hui, an envoy in China's London embassy has warned that excluding Huawei would send a "very negative message to Chinese investors" not to mention retaliation. He added by saying: "If you want to trade with China then trade with Huawei" … it was "not the time to shut the door" … and the UK did not want to "send that message at the time of Brexit"[31]

Britain is also under pressure not to use Huawei's 5G technology after agreeing to buy non-core elements from the Chinese company for its own network—subject to security issues.

[29] https://www.ft.com/content/a91825e2-8e17-11e9-a24d-b42f641eca37.

[30] Donald Trump and US officials indicated that no sector of the UK economy (including the NHS) can be excluded.

[31] *Daily Telegraph*, Saturday 22 June 2019.

The US government are aware that the British National Cyber security Centre in conjunction with the Intelligence agencies have carried out a thorough review to ensure security in any roll-out of a 5G network. But this has not influenced their decision to ban US companies from using Huawei's technology expecting its "allies" to follow suit.

In late June, Trump reportedly agreed to ease those restrictions as part of a deal to resume trade talks with China. But so far, a reversal of the blanket ban on Huawei has not occurred, and a comprehensive solution to trade tensions is at best in its very early stages, and at worst still fundamentally at odds with the aims and ambitions of the nationalist and protectionist Trump regime.[32] Furthermore, the company is aware that it cannot depend on a healthy long-term relationship with the USA, whatever now happens. "President Trump's softening stance on Huawei is an important lifeline for the company," says Dan Wang, technology analyst at Gavekal Dragonomics, a research firm. "Nonetheless, Huawei will try to design out US components and continue to build its own capabilities. It can't allow its survival to be contingent on US political actions."[33] This understanding is the actions of the USA in this trade war and reflects its wide-ranging ramifications beyond simply the Huawei dispute: namely in the way that multinational companies and states exposed to the US-Chinese supply chain will be forced to plan their business, technology and trade objectives.

How Much Is China Is Investing in the EU?

In recent years, Chinese direct investment in the Eurozone was up 37% in 2015, rising to $17.1 billion from $12.5 billion but with investment continuing to decline in 2018. Apart from Greece (as discussed above), Italy, one of the Eurozone's weaker economies, received the most investment of any EU nation from Chinese companies. That was largely down to a $7.9 billion deal between Pirelli and ChemChina. France holds second place

[32]https://www.bloomberg.com/news/articles/2019-06-25/u-s-set-to-delay-more-china-tariffs-as-talks-expected-to-resume.

[33]https://www.ft.com/content/a6db14d8-9993-11e9-9573-ee5cbb98ed36.

with $3.6 billion of investment in the tourism industry and infrastructure sectors.[34]

There are continued concerns in Brussels over China's economic ambitions which have encouraged the use of the terms "systemic rival" and "strategic competitor." China's *actual* ownership of EU businesses is by comparison relatively small, but has grown rapidly in the last ten years. A new mechanism is now in place for screening foreign investment sanctioning the EU Commission, to give an opinion when an investment "threatens the security or public order" of more than one member state or undermines an EU-wide project such as the Galileo satellite project.[35]

Particular concerns lie with the dangers of Intellectual Property theft or loss. On 1 June 2018, almost a year before Trump's Huawei ban, the European Union launched WTO legal complaints against China's alleged forced ownership-granting and usage of technology—claiming that it both discriminated against foreign firms and undermined the intellectual property rights of EU companies, which are allegedly only allowed to access Chinese markets through joint ventures.

"Technological innovation and know-how is the bedrock of our knowledge-based economy. It's what keeps our companies competitive in the global market and supports hundreds of thousands of jobs across Europe. We cannot let any country force our companies to surrender this hard-earned knowledge at its border," European Commissioner for Trade Cecilia Malmstrom stated in a press briefing on the issue, noting that such technology transfers are against WTO rules, particularly the World Trade Organization agreement on Trade-Related Aspects of Intellectual Property Rights signed by member nations in 1995, including China.[36]

More broadly, a report by Brussels 13 March 2019 calculates that a third of the EU bloc's total assets are now in the hands of foreign-owned, non-EU companies. 9.6% of companies had their ownership based in China, Hong Kong or Macau—almost quadrupling from just 2.5% in 2007, right before the financial crisis. That compares with 29% controlled by

[34] https://www.ft.com/content/c1155e72-e5e0-11e5-a09b-1f8b0d268c39.

[35] https://www.bbc.co.uk/news/world-47886902.

[36] https://www.theepochtimes.com/european-union-files-wto-complaint-against-china-on-unfair-intellectual-property-practices_2548925.html.

US and Canadian interests by the end of 2016—down from nearly 42% in 2007.[37] Cecilia **Malmström noted that**:

> This report provides a comprehensive overview of investment into the EU and reveals some important trends that we need to consider carefully. Europe benefits a lot from an open investment policy but we must be ready to act where our security and public interest are at risk. Together with the new framework on the screening of foreign direct investments we are now better equipped and better informed to deal with these types of scenarios in the future.[38]

Approach to New Deals

President Macron is encouraging member states to "Europeanize" their China policies: noting that some—such as Italy and Greece[39]—are slipping into a more bilateral mode of conduct in their determination to attract Chinese inward investment. The French president's meeting with Chinese President Xi Jinping in Paris in March 2019 was also attended by Chancellor Merkel and included the EU Commission President, thereby linking an intergovernmental meeting with the formal institutions of the EU. This was a way of ensuring that EU officials could witness meetings with top-level Chinese delegations to monitor and co-ordinate strategic approaches and oversee agreements. Germany and France have a broad *consensus ad idem on* relations with China and, unlike the USA, they not only see primarily the geopolitical threat of China's economic growth, but also envisage the ongoing opportunity this presents. Consequently, their prime objective is to strengthen the partnership, as long as it can be enacted on mutually beneficial terms.

The EU, no doubt, shares concerns about Chinese global activities. But it is equally alarmed by US policies under the Trump administration. From European eyes, the USA is increasingly seen to behave like a rogue

---

[37] http://trade.ec.europa.eu/doclib/press/index.cfm?id=1993.

[38] http://trade.ec.europa.eu/doclib/press/index.cfm?id=1993.

[39] Greece joined the "16+1" group of eastern European countries looking to deepen ties with Beijing.

superpower, hostile to the fundamental norms of international cooperation and a trading system based on multilateral agreement and binding international rules, codes and norms. Many officials argue that Trump, by design or indifference, has already badly weakened the foundation of the transatlantic relationship that American presidents have nurtured since the end of the Second World War and the formation of NATO. As Sigmar Gabriel, a former German foreign minister, put it: "He has done damage that the Soviets would have dreamt of."[40]

Nevertheless, and with these reservations about the USA aside, there has been mounting resistance in Brussels, the USA and Australia, to the growing size and volume of Chinese acquisitions. In the middle of 2015, nearly 40 billion dollars' worth of mergers and acquisitions were put on hold because of competition and issues of national security. These investments don't include the proposed takeovers of Syngenta, the Swiss Agribusiness (44 billion dollars) and Aixtron, the German semiconductor company (670 million euros), which are still being scrutinized by the regulators.[41] These concerns apart, genuine reciprocity (by the Chinese) for foreign investment will help to quell criticism. The OECD has China placed next to bottom in "restrictiveness" towards foreign direct investment in a list of 59 countries ranked.[42]

China is now a cornerstone of the global community and international trade, and together with other major economic powers this makes it prey to international market instability, exchange rates volatility and ongoing banking crises. This means it needs to work with its global partners as much as it can simply control the flux of international forces.

The EU recognizes the importance of China's increasing economic dominance, and the way in which it is being utilized to gain access to European markets by way of inward investment. The *quid pro quo* for the EU is not only economic but by continuing to insist that China engages in the introduction of political and social reforms. It is important for the EU to press on helping China establish an open democracy and civil society based

[40] https://www.washingtonpost.com/politics/europeans-fear-trump-may-threaten-not-just-the-transatlantic-bond-but-the-state-of-their-union/2019/02/04/a874e9f4-25ad-11e9-81fd-b7b05d5bed90_story.html?utm_term=.44ab9f7e2808.

[41] https://www.ft.com/topics/themes/Mergers_&_Acquisitions.

[42] http://www.oecd.org/corporate/mne/statistics.htm.

on the rule of law. There will be setbacks—such as the latest crackdown on human rights lawyers, with prominent lawyers and activists having been imprisoned for "subversion", thereby sending out a signal that anyone using the legal system to right judicial wrongs or defend human rights will themselves be punished.[43] There will be no improvement until the justice system is divorced from the communist party, with separate advocacy rights for lawyers and the establishment of the formalized independence of the judiciary.[44]

The EU's China Policy can be summarized as follows:

- To engage China further, both bilaterally and on the world stage, through an upgraded political dialogue.
- To support China's transition to an open society based upon the rule of law and respect for human rights.
- To encourage the integration of China in the world economy through bringing it fully into the world trading system, and by supporting the process of economic and social reform that is continuing in China.
- To raise the EU's profile in China.[45]

China and the EU Without Britain

The EU is China's largest trading partner but is concerned about the level of influence it can sustain if the UK leaves the EU. Brexit, if and when it finally occurs, could affect China's strategy in dealing with the EU, which has started to lean towards protectionist policies (see above). Without the support of Britain, which has been a staunch advocate of an investment pact between the EU and China, it would have to make extra efforts to boost ties with European Union countries. This is a view held by He Weiwen, co-director of the China-US-EU Study Centre Association of International Trade (which is part of the Ministry of Commerce), who has stated that "The European Union [without the presence of Britain] is likely

---

[43] https://www.ft.com/content/22b8a356-6470-11e6-8310-ecf0bddad227.

[44] Ibid.

[45] http://eeas.europa.eu/delegations/china/eu_china/political_relations/index_en.htm.

to adopt a more protectionist approach when dealing with China. [The cooperation between China and the EU] may become more difficult…. For Chinese companies which have set up headquarters or branches in the UK, they may not be able to enjoy tariff-free access to the wider European market after Britain leaves the EU."[46]

Between 2000 and 2016, Britain was a top European destination for Chinese outbound direct investment, with cumulative investments of US$16.6 billion, according to the US-based Brookings Institution. It is also the second largest trading partner with China inside the EU. A report on 17 September undertaken by Manchester Airport suggests that post-Brexit Britain may well continue to attract Chinese investment—independent of China's other initiatives (OBOR) in SE Europe. The value of inward investments was highlighted at a launch of the report by Richard Burn the UK Trade Commissioner for China, when he argued that:

> UK-China bilateral trade links have never been stronger: in 2017 UK-China bilateral trade expanded by 15.1% to reach a record £67.5bn, whilst UK exports of goods and services to China grew by 28.5%. This report demonstrates the clear benefits of direct UK-China linkages for facilitating flows of trade, investment and people between our two countries. I'm delighted to see Manchester and the surrounding region benefit so much from this flight connection to Beijing.

A more sober review had been voiced by CK Hutchison chairman Li Ka-shing, Hong Kong's richest man and leading investor in the UK, when interviewed by Bloomberg immediately before the 2016 June referendum, in which he suggested that if Britain left the EU it would be "detrimental to the UK, and it will have a negative impact to the whole of Europe".[47] As a result, Li Ka-shing said he would scale back his investment in the UK—amounting to around US$50 billion in Britain since 1995.[48] "China will probably not give up entirely on the UK, but it will treat it as what it

[46]http://www.scmp.com/news/china/diplomacy-defence/article/1978486/how-will-china-be-affected-if-britain-leaves-european.

[47]http://www.bloomberg.com/news/articles/2016-06-20/billionaire-li-ka-shing-warns-against-brexit-as-referendum-looms.

[48]http://www.scmp.com/news/china/diplomacy-defence/article/1978486/how-will-china-be-affected-if-britain-leaves-european.

will be: a medium-sized economy with a strong financial focus and not much of an industry left," said Philippe Le Corre, a researcher with the Brookings Institution and co-author of *China's Offensive in Europe*, a book published last month.[49]

This view is gaining ground. But there is no doubt London's financial hub would remain important to Chinese investors as a renminbi trading hub. This was the first step for deciding the future UK_EU relationship. It was endorsed by EU leaders at a special meeting of the European Council on the 25 November 2018—the first step in the transitional (Brexit) future trade negotiations.[50]

Nevertheless, business sentiment overall has been dampened by the continued uncertainty posed by the failure of the UK legislature to sign off the EU- UK "Withdrawal Agreement and Political Declaration", and the corresponding uncertainty surrounding whether Brexit will be delayed, rejected altogether, or delivered in the form of a "no-deal" crashing out of the EU—as Boris Johnson, the leading candidate for UK Prime Minister in the Tory party elections, has said is acceptable to deliver on the 2016 referendum. Such uncertainty may have cost the economy as much as £600 million a week, according to one Goldman Sachs report of April 2019.[51]

China's Reserve Currency Status

The focus on the EU as a reserve currency was long considered (in Chapter 3 of this book) as a counterweight to the dollar's supremacy in world trade. But China's Renminbi (RMB) formally became a reserve currency on 1 October 2016—an event which follows years of lobbying by the Chinese authorities, and coincides with the 67th anniversary of the commencement of communist rule. This means the RMB is to be incorporated in the International Monetary Fund's special drawing rights

---

[49]Brookings Institution Press, 17 May 2016.

[50]The UK Parliament rejected the Withdrawal Agreement 3× delaying Brexit until 29 October 2019.

[51]https://uk.reuters.com/article/uk-britain-eu-goldmansachs/brexit-uncertainty-has-cost-britain-600-million-a-week-goldman-sachs-idUKKCN1RD1T8.

(SDR)—a reserve asset class whose value was previously determined by a basket of just the dollar, euro, yen and pound sterling. This in practice means it falls behind the dollar (66%) and the Euro (20%) as the world's third reserve currency—dislodging sterling from that position. This should support the removal of domestic opposition to currency reforms and pave the way for further restructuring of its economy from export—led to domestic growth. Reserve currency status for the RMBs (10.92%) weighting adds to its growing influence in trade with the EU and the rest of the world.[52]

Christine Lagarde, IMF managing director (and nominated for president of the ECB), said the inclusion of the renminbi in the SDR basket was a recognition of the progress China had made in reforming its monetary, foreign exchange and financial systems as well as advances liberalizing its financial markets.

"The extension of the SDR basket is a historical milestone for the SDR, for the fund but more importantly for China and the international monetary system," she said. "It is an important step in the integration of the Chinese economy into the global financial and monetary system."[53]

The EU's problems with mass migration, a faltering Eurozone and the instability caused by Brexit will require China to modify its own strategic outlook on Europe. In contrast, the EU looks to China to partner in building a safer and securer global economic environment—*a level playing field* between the two trading blocs working together to further their mutual interests; for innovation cooperation, including reciprocal admission to respective research and innovation programmes.

Broadly speaking then, EU–China cooperation is progressing on a wide front. The EU-China Strategic Agenda 2020 provides a common framework for this EU-China cooperation, highlighting new fields of collaboration increasing their roles and responsibilities as global players. Furthermore, foreign and security policies have become a major aspect of EU-China relations. The EU and China have played a constructive role in

[52]1 October 2016, the RMB officially received reserve currency status with a 10.92% weighting in the IMFs Special Drawing Rights. The Chinese RMB was finally, included in the IMF's basket of reserve currencies in December 2015.

[53]https://www.ft.com/content/2baa6fec-86d2-11e6-bcfc-debbef66f80e.

fighting piracy off the coast of Somalia (in the Horn of Africa), and overall in the fight against international terrorism. Conditions for successful cooperation activities of mutual benefit exist for both sides.

Assumptions about China's domestic reform trajectory and its international ambitions have changed fundamentally. While EU member states engage with China to varying degrees, few now dispute that its rise is based on an authoritarian party system, massive state intervention in the economy and an uneven playing field for foreign competitors. In the light of the ongoing US–China trade war, and growing British and European concerns about intellectual property theft and potential spying and network infiltration via Chinese technology firms, these concerns about the characteristics of Chinese capitalism and state power have gained a new and harder edge to them.

7

Reinvigorating the EU Project

Setting the record straight; "ever closer union"; reforms; the new EU Commission President's agenda; the "Brussels effect"; reinvigorating the Currency Union; EU Soft Power.

The question of how to reinvigorate the European project will concentrate the minds of EU politicians even more now that the European Parliamentary elections have (just) taken place. With the old centre-left and centre-right hegemony no longer in place, the political complexion of the EU Parliament will be more fluid and unpredictable. Populist parties have increased their support but not to the extent expected while the green and liberals parties increased representation. The UK's participation—however temporary—exposed turmoil in British politics with the recently formed Brexit party creaming off 31.6% of the UK vote and sending 29 MEPs to Brussels. Brexit and the recently formed Brexit "populist" party have been a wake-up call not just for EU Institutions, but for all governments

J. Theodore, *Survival of the European (Dis) Union*,
https://doi.org/10.1007/978-3-030-31214-5_7

within the EU.[1] Jean-Claude Junker's ambitious mandate for recharging the EU on taking office in 2014 is still a work in progress. It was not able to absorb recent political traumas, such as the rise in populism which followed in recent domestic elections and gave populist mandates in Italy and Central Europe, together with a strong parliamentary representation in other nations.

This chapter aims to set the record straight on what has been achieved in the EU, both long term and in recent years, and examines those issues, however challenging, which remain to be addressed. On 17 May 2019, at an EU Summit in Sibiu, Romania, national leaders made a renewed commitment to an EU that delivers on the issues that really matter to people. But to win back voters, this means new policies to ease concerns over migration, promote innovation and inclusive growth and write a new social contract that ensures a sustainable welfare state across Europe for the twenty-first century.

The Christian Democratic leader (CDU), Annegret Kramp-Karrenbauer, captured the mood of voters when she spoke at a rally on 19 May saying that Europe "must not bother with the little things" but instead focus on the "big issues – freedom and security". And security meant above all "protecting" the EU's external borders—the very essence of the current populists' message in the EU Parliamentary elections.

The EU is trying to claim some progress on its 2014–2019 agenda but as Jean-Claude Junker EU Commission President stated in a State of the Union address (September 2017), "We started to fix the European roof. But today and tomorrow we must patiently, floor by floor, moment by moment, inspiration by inspiration, continue to add new floors to the European House. We must complete the European House now that the sun is shining and whilst it still is…We now have a window of opportunity but it will not stay open forever… Let us make the most of the momentum, catch the wind in our sails".

But does the rhetoric capture enough of the new political reality—namely that voters want action to improve their lives: but without the

[1]The impact of Brexit will vary considerably across the European Union, with some regions bracing for severe costs and others less exposed. The impact of the Brexit party in the EU elections is having profound effect on the British two-party system with right-wing conservatives. dominating the political agenda.

consequence of a larger, more centralized bureaucracy reminiscent of a so-called nanny state. Electorates have become more concerned with the preservation of their culture, national and regional identity under perceived threat from uncontrolled migration. This means bringing the refugee crisis under control and making the allocation of refugees within Europe entirely voluntary for individual nations. Member states should not be forced to accept asylum seekers and refugees they ultimately don't want and nor should refugees be forced to settle in countries where they don't feel welcome or don't want to go.[2] Implementing a realistic and transparent plan that meets these concerns would help to dampen the populist cause. Unscrupulous populist politicians have been highly successful in exploiting resentment, but offer no realistic panaceas for voters pressing concerns on how they would tackle economic and welfare issues.

Helle Thorning-Schmidt, CEO Save the Children International and former Prime Minister of Denmark, agreed on the need for Europe to respond to voters' worries over migration, while reaffirming its values in supporting minority rights, defending the social market economy and enabling welfare. "We have an obligation to work for a Europe of the future for our children, we have to hand a Europe to our children that is better than we have today", Thorning-Schmidt said. "If you want to solve something at a national level, you often need a European solution", she added. "We need to step up and we need to solve the problems we are facing, and the time is now".[3]

Reform of the Dublin Regulations and a review of the Schengen agreement may be required for this.[4] So far, uncontrolled immigration has put an unfair burden on Italy and Greece both blighted by the burden of Eurozone austerity. It is no wonder that public resentment has fuelled the recent growth of Matteo Salvini's Lega party in a coalition government with the Five Star Movement in Italy, not to mention a hard right

---

[2]Poland and Hungary and other Central EU states wish to preserve ethnicity and oppose the development of multiculturalism.

[3]https://www.friendsofeurope.org/sites/default/files/media-files/soe_report_2018.pdf.

[4]*Dublin 111 Regulation* (Regulation604/2013) sets out the criteria and mechanisms of determining which member states is responsible for dealing with the request of international protection presented by a third country national or stateless person in one of the EU member states.

The Schengen Area covers 26 EU states without internal borders for free and unrestricted movement but with common rules on control of external borders.

resurgence through the Vox party in Spain. Renewing citizens confidence will start by action to protect its external borders, albeit to leave open an entry opportunity for lawful migrants. Member states, in turn, must not close off their internal borders except in times of emergency—for example when clamping down on international terrorism. The idea of a "fortress Europe" closed to both political refugees and economic migrants not only violates European and international law—hard borders in the modern world are also totally unrealistic, being both impractical to enforce, and self-defeating, when we consider the vital role new migrants play in the economies of Europe.

The burning question is whether the new EU Parliament will reinvigorate the bloc's capacity to address these challenges. It certainly has a vital role to play. The new EU Parliament has gained an influx of right-wing nationalists and nativists trying to unite under a nationalist banner that had been touted by Matteo Salvini in his campaign rhetoric as a plan to fight for a "Europe of common sense". Their election agenda had focused on the EU's three key, pressing problems: an austerity policy that has hampered Europe's economic development; the refugee crisis and its associated political fallout; and the territorial challenges and threat of disintegration exemplified by Brexit. Eurosceptic parties have signalled they want to disrupt the status quo but remain pro-Europe. This distinguishes their brand of Euroscepticism from Brexit. Up to now, the EU Parliament has been dominated by the "Grand Coalition" of the centre-right European People's Party and the Social democrats (S&D), which favour greater European Integration. The increase (though less than expected) in MEPs from the new populist parties promoting national agendas will—if they are able to form a united alliance—help to quash any further moves in that direction. Voters need to know their views are being voiced in the only directly elected democratic chamber. This will renew confidence that decisions of both the Executive and the European Council can be challenged by the Parliament.

"Ever Closer Union"

At a State of the Union address by EU Commission, President Jean-Claude Junker in Strasbourg on 13 September 2017 acknowledged urgent action is needed to reinforce the benefits of membership with voters. But apart from the most ardent "federalists", the mood for further EU Integration is simply not on the menu. Nationalistic governments in Eastern Europe, as well as right-wing populist movements in Austria, Germany and Italy, have sent a clear message to Brussels to accommodate the needs of ordinary citizens and communicate why there is no enthusiasm for more integration. In one of President Junker's key messages, entitled "Better Regulation", he stated that: "We should not meddle in the everyday lives of European citizens ... We should not march in with a stream of new initiatives or seek ever growing competences. We should give back competences to member states where it makes sense".[5] He went on to state that "I will be setting up a Subsidiarity and Proportionality Task Force as of this month to take a very critical look at all policy areas to make sure we are only acting where the EU adds value".

Junker may have been playing to the gallery, but this was precisely the kind of language to draw interest from EU members—especially those critical of the whole principle and goal of "ever closer union". Beata Szydlo, the Polish Prime Minister, reflecting the views her Visegrád neighbours (namely the Czech Republic, Hungary and Slovakia), stated that:

> People in Europe feel more and more that the elites in Brussels are no longer in touch with the problems that they should be concerned about — such as the safety of the citizens of the EU, the labour situation, and increasing employment and improving wages... They are more and more focused on the bureaucracy, and on the red tape that they have themselves created ... This leads to crisis and ... we should discuss these matters especially now after the UK decided to leave the EU.[6]

---

[5]http://europa.eu/rapid/press-release_IP-17-3164_en.htm.

[6]https://www.ft.com/content/05942108-c55c-11e7-a1d2-6786f39ef675.

Ursula von der Leyen—A New Agenda

Meeting expectations of EU citizens will take on a new urgency when the new EU Parliament starts afresh after the summer recess and Ursula von der Leyen, the new EU Commission President, takes up her appointment on 1 November. Her citizens will want an agenda that incorporates all the policies that Brussels *can* develop and which influence their future economic welfare and well-being. Ms. Leyen, to secure her approval (by the EU Parliament), presented an ambitious 24-page "policy framework" that championed environmental issues, social policies and gender equality. Her success—by a narrow majority of nine votes—came with the support of the far-right and anti-establishment MEPs from Italy, Poland and Hungary.

The latter (two) were determined to block Frans Timmermans, an EU Commission Vice-President who as guardian of the rule of law had been at the forefront of their quarrel with Brussels. But this cannot assume Ms. Leyen will go soft with EU states on rule breaking and erosion of democratic principles.[7] On migration, however, she *has* expressed a more considerate view saying that:

> "The migration issue will be with us for decades", and that EU countries such as Poland or Hungary, who have rebelled against migrant-sharing quotas with Greece and Italy, ought to be "listened to", she said.
>
> "I put the case of Poland, with its argument that they have already welcomed 1.5m Ukrainians. Ukraine is a country with a hybrid war, for years, in which people are still dying. We cannot ignore it", she explained.[8]

There is of course more than altruism in Poland's accepting so many Ukrainian migrants apart from affinities in religion and culture traditions. Poland has a critical labour shortage. Since joining the EU in 2004, it has experienced a vast outflow of skilled workers to the UK and other Western Europe destinations. Ukraine migrants have helped to fill shortages in the labour market particularly in the building industries. This is where EU Structural Funds have focused on Poland's infrastructure especially roads

[7] "Article 7" is a political weapon used as part of a legal process that can lead to a member state being punished if found to have breached the bloc's core values.

[8] https://euobserver.com/news/145504.

and railways which have been considerably upgraded helping the economy to grow faster than other EU economies.

But to drive her agenda forward, Ursula von der Leyen will need as much cross-party support as she can get even from those who have in recent years damaged relations with Brussels over treatment of refugees and the erosion of democracy and the rule of law. The attempt to repair relations by Hungary may well be connected to potential threats by the EU Commission to link the level of future EU Structural funding to each beneficiary country's record on upholding democratic principles. Charges of a drift to autocratic rule have been levelled against Fidesz, Viktor Orban ruling party in Budapest. A loss of funds would be important for Hungary as EU funding currently amounts to almost 3.5% of Hungary's gross national income.

Its foreign minister, Mr. Szijjarto in a conciliatory tone, has stated that he was certain Hungary would "have debates" with Mrs. von der Leyen, adding: "We consider it as natural, because the European Union is faced with historic types of challenges — so why shouldn't we have debates?" "With Ursula von der Leyen we have a good hope that these debates will be based on mutual respect, and that's why we have support for her".[9]

In Poland, the leading conservative newspaper "Rzeszpospolita" revealed that *all* the country's ruling Law and Justice Party (PiS) MEPs backed Ms. Leyen, the former defence minister of Germany. The paper expressed the hope that "the new European Commission will not resume the ideological crusade, which [Dutch Socialist] Frans Timmermans ran", and that "Brussels will abandon all its fantasies about the formation of a European army and the weakening of Nato".[10] Poland is a staunch supporter of NATO and has lobbied for a permanent presence of US forces within its borders as a bulwark against Russia's continued interference not only in Ukraine but also in the Baltics.

On the issue of working towards a United States of Europe, there is clear departure from her predecessor. Ms. Leyen signals a change of heart from her former federalist approach. This will help to calm fears of friction with new-found supporters as well as populists and right-wing governments

[9]https://www.ft.com/content/e568cb3c-a9a6-11e9-b6ee-3cdf3174eb89?.

[10]https://www.bbc.co.uk/news/world-europe-49017291.

throughout the EU. Her dream of a federalized EU has become "more mature and more realistic".

"In the European Union, there is unity in diversity", she added. "That's different from federalism. I think that's the right way". Broadly speaking, she captures the mood that "ever closer (political) union" is off the table.

Multilateralism—EU Relations with China and the USA

What EU Parliamentarians still await (and expect) to hear is the new EU Commission's developing policy on plans to protect multilateralism especially in the context of global trade. Ms. Leyen has not revealed a strategy on how the EU should position itself between the USA and China their current tariff trade war. Nor is there any indication on tackling EU industrial and competition policy—a policy that is currently focused on a consumer—welfare approach at what some say is at the expense of food safety and consumer protection.[11] There is no statement on endorsing further EU enlargement or find consensus in the union's vexed negotiations over its long-term budget.

As a sounding board for official US reaction to her appointment Gordon Sonderland, the US ambassador to the EU remarks that: "It gives the United States and the European Union an opportunity to reset its entire relationship", adding that: " things have begun to stagnate a little. They've begun to reach impasses on a number of fronts".

> And I think a changing of the guard, if you will, would be healthy for the relationship. And we will be able to start with a clean sheet of paper.

The relationship between the USA and the EU has been fraught over recent years, notably on trade, climate change and the Iran nuclear deal.[12]

---

[11]www.socialeurope.eu; EU competition policy: a more holistic approach needed Magdalena Senn, 28 March 2019.

[12]https://www.euronews.com/2019/07/20/new-eu-chief-von-der-leyen-will-allow-brussels-and-washington-to-reset-relationship?utm_source=newsletter&utm_medium=en&utm_content=new-eu-chief-von-der-leyen-will-allow-brussels-and-washington-to-reset-relationship.

With the UK gone (if Brexit takes effect on 31 October 2019), there will be no British veto. What recent Brexit negotiations have shown is that the Commission does not create policy—but has the charge of initiating it. This is driven by the increasing role of national leaders meeting as the European Council which actively decides collective EU policy. This has been clearly demonstrated in the Brexit negotiations. It is the EU Council which has agreed decisions on allowing Brexit delays—not Commission bureaucrats or EU Parliamentarians. For years, the British media and politicians frequently complain about decisions of "unelected Brussels bureaucrats" and the "meddling European superstate" when in reality it is the democratically elected national leaders in the EU Council that make all the important decisions.[13] The Council is scheduled under the Lisbon Treaty to meet six or seven times a year, but recent crises have increased the need to meet more often. In addition, the Eurogroup of finance ministers usually meets monthly to discuss Eurozone matters.

Critics of the EU have singled out a lack of democracy in its workings—a term referred to as the "democratic deficit".[14] But does it make laws? No, although it does make proposals (many of which come via national political leaders) which are then deliberated, amended and passed or rejected by the elected representatives of national governments and directly elected members of the European Parliament.[15] It has political leadership functions as well as more administrative ones. As the civil service of a supernational organization, it represents the EU in trade agreements like CETA signed with Canada. Lack of transparency is as much the fault of EU member states not informing its electorate sufficiently—through the educational system—on what it stands for and merits of membership. Ignorance of the EU is almost universal. A filtered, distorted and inaccurate version of the relevance of its various institutions, and on how control is devolved, is widespread. Myths about the EU as a form engineered authoritarianism are rampant and exploited by populists and nationalist wholesale.

With the creation of the Eurozone from 1999 and the enlargement of the EU since 2004, it has become even more important to explain its

[13]The EU Council meets 6–7 times a year but recently more often and the Eurogroup of finance ministers usually meets monthly, and the Foreign Affairs Council of foreign ministers at least that.

[14]A term used by the British political scientist Professor David Marquand in 1979.

[15]MEPs are elected by proportional representation.

importance to EU citizens. Are all EU "bureaucrats" in the Commission all powerful and unaccountable—as is perceived to be the case?[16] Do they only represent the forces of a neoliberal ruling elite present? Many would say *yes*, a perception held by Eurosceptics and even by pro-Europeans generally. But perceptions of remoteness, bureaucracy and perceived lack of transparency are often criticisms that can be levelled at any "Whitehall" (London) style state institution—whether, for example, Fonction Publique Francaise (in Paris) or the Deutscher Beamtenbund (in Berlin).[17]

Rejecting the status quo, however, falls short of member states questioning their support for the Union per se. Crisis management in recent years has demanded a more proactive role for the European Council where at times the biggest players speak the loudest but even the smallest have their say. Increasingly "The Union is not a state but a union of states",[18] where key "elected" political figures influence the decisions that affect the stability and survival of the project. This helps to diminish (but not extinguish) the argument that there is a "democratic deficit" in EU decision-making. It wasn't Michel Barnier (EU Brexit negotiator) or Guy Verhofstadt (EU Parliament Brexit coordinator) who argued against a long Brexit delay but President Macron. Macron made sure the extension was short foreseeing potential disruption in the EU Elections. In 2015, it was Germany's "elected" finance minister Wolfgang Schäuble, and not the EU Commission, who stood firm on the terms of Greece's bailout rescue package demanding massive privatization sale of Greek assets vehemently opposed by the Greek government at the time.[19] It is important for voters to believe the (EU) Commission executes policy and is answerable to both EU Parliament and Council of Ministers. This will demonstrate that democracy is at work and encourage renewed confidence in the democratic process.

Winning back voters to the European cause is a task that Brussels will find difficult without using the very weapons of digital technology and social media that recently were so successfully utilized by populist parties

---

[16]Legislative proposals do emanate from the Commission but they have to be considered by the Council of Ministers in conjunction with MEPs who are elected directly by EU citizens.

[17]The European Union and the Eurozone under Stress (2017) John Theodore, Jonathan Theodore with Dimitrios Syrrakos.

[18]Luuk Van Middelaar in "Alarums and Excursions" 2019.

[19]https://www.guardian.com/bisiness/2015/jul/12.

in Europe and the USA. The EU has failed to boast of its achievements in ways that can be understood by ordinary citizens. The resurgence of the old European "spirit of solidarity" is largely in their hands. Clearly, the EU needs to improve its public relations. For too long, EU governments press and media have used the EU as a scapegoat for short-term political gain. The EU policymakers have taken for granted that Europeans will see the benefits of integration. Reaching out to EU citizens is now seen as a new opportunity to improve citizens' lives, but also to explain to the general public what is actually been *done.*[20] This has to be done as populist forces prepare their battle lines for orchestrating populist agendas in a future EU Parliament. They are expected to secure important gains; to demand far-reaching reforms; the return of power to domestic national governments and the reversal of shared sovereignty partially (but in no way comprehensively) surrendered by EU club membership.

Global Role—The Brussels Effect

The EU has the world's largest internal market and one protected by strong regulatory institutions. This provides benefits for EU consumers in that imported goods both food and manufactured goods from outside the bloc must satisfy stringent regulatory tests. This shields EU economies from cheap imports especially from heavily industrialized production methods and adulterated foodstuffs which threaten to undercut European farmers. British trade negotiators racing round the world under the banner of "Global Britain" are already experiencing these regulatory challenges/issues in preliminary UK–US trade discussions. The USA in any future Free Trade Agreement (FTA) will insist on the UK accepting farm goods such as GM crops, "chlorinated" chicken and hormone-injected beef as part of any comprehensive agreement—but this will not be popular with a more discerning British public, accustomed to foodstuffs produced and delivered under stricter EU rules.

EU consumers and their domestic industries are shielded by an internal market and their relative competitive position in the global economy.

[20]https://e.europa.eu/beta-political/ files a report by Luc Van den Brande October 2017.

Brexit UK welcomes a future when it can sign its own free trade agreements, but bilateral deals will inevitably reduce its bargaining power with the big economies like the USA, India and China—a problem that the EU can match having the negotiating base of 500 million consumers. European consumers will expect Brussels to exert its global status against a hostile trading environment being conducted by the USA. The tariff war between the USA and China will have an adverse impact on the world economy, as all major economists have pointed out. This makes the role of the EU bloc vital in protecting multilateral agreements and the fundamental rules of the international trading structure.

While the EU regulates only its internal market, multinational corporations become incentivized by its regulatory framework, for both politics and profit margins, to standardize their production globally and follow a single rule—which transforms EU regulation into an effectively global one. EU rules have ended up dictating what kind of air conditioners Americans use to cool their homes and why their children no longer find soft plastic toys in their McDonald's Happy Meals. This phenomenon creates what is widely known as a de facto "Brussels Effect". Furthermore, once these firms have adjusted their business practices to meet the EU's strict standards and absorbed the costs for doing so, they then have the incentive to lobby their domestic governments to adopt these same standards to level the playing field against their domestic, non-export-oriented competitors. This is the Brussels Effect in action.[21]

The Brussels Effect and the European Digital Single Market

Facebook and many other companies are having to update their privacy policies and service terms to comply with EU legislation governing data and privacy. This is part of a sweeping overhaul of digital privacy laws being implemented from May 2018 that will force changes on how technology companies handle customer data that creates for a de jure for the European Union but a de-facto global standard giving the US citizens

[21]Article by Professor Anu Bradford "The Brussels Effect" Northwestern University School of Law Printed in the USA. Northwestern University Law Review Vol. 107, No. 1.

new protections as well.[22] The cornerstone of this is collectively known as GDPR, standing for General Data Protection Regulation, which gives users the right to demand the deletion of data and to object to new forms of data collection. At the same time, the new rules require that companies obtain unequivocal consent for how they collect, process and use data attracting fines for breaches of up to 4% of global profits. On this, the EU can rightly claim leadership in setting standards which no doubt others will follow. "The path to privacy in the United States has to be fought through Europe", said Jeff Chester, executive director of the Centre for Digital Democracy, a privacy watchdog group.[23]

G7 and Big Tech

Taxing "Big Tech" has recently attracted the attention of the USA particularly its tensions with France who wish to impose a 3% turnover tax levy on tech businesses hitting mainly American corporations.[24] EU governments are critical that multinationals have not been paying their fair share of company tax in the states where they operate. This is because they can (still) register profits in low-tax "havens" jurisdictions such as Ireland Luxembourg or the Channel Islands. The USA acknowledges there should be concerted action on this.

At the recent G7 July meeting in France attended by finance ministers, a compromise was agreed on how to change the international tax regime to ensure fair taxation of multinationals, including technology groups such as Google and Facebook. Steven Mnuchin, US Treasury secretary was quoted as saying: "We've made some significant progress at this meeting". But he added: "There is still work to be done". Adding that:

---

[22]Although GDPR does not directly limit how tech companies treat customers outside of Europe, the "*Brussels effect*" has some technology companies opting to adopt a single global standard, which has led to a hike in recent months to issue *new privacy policies*, tighten internal procedures and request new permissions from users. Even other companies, where data collection is not the core of their businesses, have followed suit.

[23]https://www.washingtonpost.com/business/technology/europe-not-the-us-is-now-the-most-powerful-regulator-of-silicon-valley/2018/05/25/f7dfb600-604f-11e8-8c93-8cf33c21da8d_story.html.

[24]France may abandon the national tax on digital companies if an international agreement is signed.

> "We don't have a solution", but "We're beginning to develop a framework. We feel very strongly that this should not just be geared at the US digital companies".[25]

The G7 did however agree that new rules would be established through ongoing negotiations at the Paris-based Organisation of Economic Co-Operation and Development (OECD)—"to address new business models that would deal with those creating value with no physical presence, notably highly digitalised business models".[26]

They (G7) also agreed to the principle of a global minimum corporate tax rate. This would help to ensure by making it less attractive for multinationals to divert profits to tax havens or low-tax jurisdictions and deny tax revenues to those states where they generate revenues.

The EU—Taxing Big Tech

On top of this, the EU offers mechanisms for dealing with tax avoidance in its legal forms. The main principles of tax law in the EU have been from its outset that there was "no need for an across the board harmonization of member states' tax systems"... and that "member states are free to choose the tax systems that they consider most appropriate for and according to their preferences' subject to EU rules which in turn must satisfy the principle of subsidiarity and proportionality.[27]

However, while taxation *in principle* remains the preserve of member states, there is an overwhelming desire to ensure that no state (within the EU) obtains an unfair advantage by special tax arrangements for organizations (and individuals) within or outside their tax jurisdiction.[28]

The central aim of EU tax policy was, and still is, to mitigate tax hurdles for cross-border economic activity and to encourage greater collaboration

---

[25] *Financial Times*, 19 July 2019.

[26] Ibid.

[27] EU Commission's tax policy strategy explained in a communication 23 March 2001 on "Tax Policy in the European Union—Priorities for the years ahead" (COM(2001)260).

[28] The tax provisions chapter (Articles 110–113) of the Treaty on the Functioning of the European Union (TFEU), which relates to the harmonization of legislation concerning turnover taxes, excise duties and other forms of indirect taxation.

between tax regimes. This challenge is in formulating how can this be done to best effect in an enlarged EU of 28 (or 27 members after Brexit).[29]

Brussels has a unique position to protect the EU consumer from some of the worst consequences of globalization and leads a robust fight against the tech sector (including Facebook) and other multinational corporations. The crusade against the multinationals began in earnest in 2012/2013. The EU continues to conduct a full-frontal attack on international conglomerates using complex tax avoidance schemes and profit shifting to mitigate their tax liabilities. Margrethe Vestager, Competition Commissioner, directs a number of high profile investigations against EU members. In a statement made on 3 December 2015, Ms. Vestager declared that Luxembourg had acted against the spirit of a US–Luxembourg double taxation treaty. "A tax ruling that agrees to McDonald's paying no tax on their European royalties either in Luxembourg or in the US has to be looked at very carefully under EU state aid rules", she said. "The purpose of double taxation treaties between countries is to avoid double taxation — not to justify double non-taxation".[30] The ruling against McDonalds following this was made in October 2015, against both Luxembourg and the Netherlands, when the Commission instructed both states to recover tens of millions of Euros in unpaid taxes from Fiat, the Italian car manufacturer, and Starbucks: both accused—as with many other companies—of aggressive tax avoidance measures.[31] In 2016, Apple was ordered to pay 13 billion Euros after EU rules found that Ireland had been in breach of EU state aid rules.[32] In a separate case, the EU ordered the UK to recover illegal tax aid from multinationals. This investigation was part of several "sweetheart" tax deals being offered by EU countries.

In her latest battle with the tech giants, Ms. Vestager has launched an investigation into Amazon and its European business practices over potential breaches of EU antitrust legislation. Specifically, it concerns Amazon

[29]The role of the EU Parliament has generally endorsed the broad lines of the Commission's programs in the field of taxation.

[30]https://www.taxjustice.net/2015/12/03/european-commission-to-probe-mcdonalds-tax-deal-with-luxembourg/.

[31]https://www.nytimes.com/2015/.../starbucks-fiat-eu-tax-netherlands-luxembourg.html.

[32]The total payment made by Apple included the principle of 13.1 million Euros plus EU interest of 1.2 million Euros.

appearing to use "competitively sensitive information" belonging to thousands of independent retailers. This new investigation will study how the use of this data affects competition, with a focus on Amazon's "buy box". This method of purchase is widely used by allowing customers to add items from a specific retailer directly into their shopping carts. The alleged temptation voiced by some is that Amazon is/has been quick to move into bestselling goods discovered by these smaller traders.

The EU Commission recognizes that "E-commerce has boosted retail competition and brought more choice and better prices", Vestager said. "We need to ensure that large online platforms don't eliminate these benefits through anti-competitive behaviour".

> I have therefore decided to take a very close look at Amazon's business practices and its dual role as marketplace and retailer, to assess its compliance with EU competition rules.[33]

The question for the EU competition office will be to gauge whether Amazon, with its dual role as seller and host, gives it an unfair advantage in being able to compete against small businesses having insider knowledge of what products sell best. This was not the first time that the EU Commission had Amazon in its sights as an earlier antitrust inquiry into Amazon's domination in the e-book market forcing it to amend clauses in its contracts. The company was also ordered to repay €250m in special tax breaks to Luxembourg.

Robust action on tax avoidance by Margrethe Vestager has done much to enhance her reputation. Tax avoidance denies revenue to domestic governments whose citizens' continue to face prolonged austerity. So it resonates with EU citizens perceiving a proactive role by Brussels working in their interest.

For the present, this tough approach is unpopular with the multinationals and ferments increasing uncertainty for these companies' tax liabilities in their established economic model based on foreign direct investment (FDI), especially if, following the Apple ruling, further investigations being

[33] https://www.theguardian.com/technology/2019/jul/17/amazon-faces-eu-inquiry-over-treatment-of-small-retailers.

conducted result in the EU issuing similar verdicts. Multinationals with their tax base in Ireland are levied corporate tax at 12.5% making it the lowest apart from Hungary in the EU. The EU Commission has extended its tax probes into a comprehensive investigation of Tax Havens—with the creation of a blacklist of those countries acting as depositories of billions of dollars of untaxed wealth that have failed to provide Brussels and domestic tax authorities with their source of corporate and private deposits.

The EU's actions will be popular with consumers but not with multinationals, who are constantly threatening to move business elsewhere.[34] But why would EU citizens be sympathetic with such companies—being aware of their own governments' problems to increase tax revenues in a period of austerity for urgent public spending needs. The populist agenda sweeping Europe has identified a linkage between the multinationals and their hold on the global economy which benefits the big players and is increasingly perceived by the electoral to be rigged in their favour, at the expense of ordinary people. Citizens have become aware and critical of large corporations stockpiling profits, with impunity, in tax havens, through complex tax avoidance measures to mitigate tax liabilities. Although not a primary issue in the Brexit decision, leave voters in the UK felt a sense of alienation from globalization, symbolized in their view by the banks and multinationals whose interests are propped up by Brussels and neoliberal regimes—especially since 2008.

Tax havens deprive governments around the world of tens of billions of dollars each year, fuelling poverty and inequality and depriving states of essential funds for infrastructure and welfare. At the same time, these EU policies increase uncertainty for these companies' tax liabilities in their European trading relations, for their future investment plans, and their future tax commitments are very difficult to accurately gauge. For member states such as Ireland, this could put at risk its long-held economic model based primarily on foreign direct investment (FDI) if, as a result of the Apple ruling, further investigations being conducted result in the EU issuing similar verdicts to other large companies. Multinationals with

[34] Apple secured a one-off tax "repatriation" deal with US revenue authorities of 15.5% on its overseas cash deposits.

their "port" base in Ireland currently enjoy corporate tax levied at 12.5%, a rate likely to be maintained throughout 2019.

Attempts to harmonize corporation tax rates in the EU are being resisted by Ireland and Hungary (with the lowest rate of 9%). "Taxation is an important component of competition", Hungarian Prime Minister Viktor Orban told a joint news conference in January 2018 with his Irish counterpart Leo Varadkar. "We would not like to see any regulation in the EU, which would bind Hungary's hands in terms of tax policy, be it corporate tax, or any other tax", Orban said. "We do not consider tax harmonization a desired direction".[35] While taxation *in principle* remains the preserve of member states, there is an overwhelming desire to ensure that no state within the EU obtains an unfair advantage by special tax arrangements for organizations (and individuals) within or outside their tax jurisdiction.[36]

The central aim of EU tax policy was, and still is, to mitigate tax hurdles for cross-border economic activity and to encourage greater collaboration/cooperation between tax regimes. The challenge is in formulating how can this be done to best effect in an enlarged EU of 28 soon to be 27 members after Brexit. Commissioner Margrethe Vestager has earned a strong reputation for her tough stance in confronting the multinationals, placing her as a joint front runner for next EU President supported by the ALDE group (Alliance of Liberals and Democrats for Europe).[37]

Reinvigorating the Currency Union

Reform of the Eurozone—something advocated by leading economists as urgent for its ultimate survival—continues to be the most pressing issue in the EU alongside than immigration. New "Europe" apart from Slovakia (and Slovenia in SE Europe) is not in the Eurozone, while Hungary and Poland are not ready to join the Euro yet are obliged to do so as per

[35]https://uk.reuters.com/article/us-hungary-ireland-taxation/hungary-ireland-oppose-eu-wide-tax-harmonization-efforts-idUKKBN1ET1ZY.

[36]The tax provisions chapter (Articles 110-113) of the Treaty on the Functioning of the European Union (TFEU), which relates to the harmonization of legislation concerning turnover taxes, excise duties and other forms of indirect taxation.

[37]https://www.thejournal.ie/european-commission-president-candidates-4633928-May2019/.

their 2004 Accession agreement. This can be avoided, for now, as their economies don't satisfy the convergence criteria. To do so, budget deficits must not exceed 3% of GDP with government debt at levels not in excess of 60% of GDP before joining.

Poland's Law and Justice Party (PiS) Chairman, Mr. Kaczynski, is threatening *not* to join the single currency until Polish salaries are comparable with those in the richer member states with more developed economies. He has made this an EU election pledge asking the pro-European opposition to support this approach, which he believes will be a vote winner. He quotes with hindsight the Eurozone debacle to date of "[The euro] works for the Germans, the Dutch, maybe you can add Austria and one or two other countries ... But others, even such big and strong countries like France, are simply losing out, and some are even falling into ruin. Greece is the best example", Mr. Kaczynski said at a party convention in Lublin, claiming that Eurozone membership risked driving up prices and leaving Poles worse off. "No matter what the mechanism of joining the euro will be, in one way or another we will lose from it ... that is why we are saying no to the euro, no to European prices".[38]

Like the other Central European nations that joined the EU in 2004, Poland is ultimately obliged to join the euro. But there is no formal deadline. Poland's growth rates are the highest in Europe, and there is little enthusiasm for dumping the strong Zloty given the crop of Euro crises of late. However, Zloty's strength does affect its competitiveness. Piotr Bujak, chief economist at PKO BP in Warsaw, said, "But I'm not sure that this outweighs the costs of being a member of the Eurozone in the next five to 10 years", pointing to the single currency's unfinished institutional framework and the lack of political agreement on fiscal union.[39] Kaczynski and the ruling Law and Justice Party need an issue that will drive Poles to the ballot box, but as in other member states, EU Parliamentary elections don't have the emotive appeal of domestic politics and low turnouts are the norm. Eurozone membership is unpopular (58% against joining), but this doesn't reflect overall enthusiasm for EU membership.

---

[38] https://www.express.co.uk/news/world/1125319/eu-poland-reject-single-currency-Jaroslaw-Kaczynski.

[39] https://www.ft.com/content/be847592-70ae-11e9-bbfb-5c68069fbd15.

Fiscal Union

Germany continually rejects the drive to fiscal union. Many Eurozone partners continue to run budget deficits (of 3%+) and public debt close to or in excess of 100% of GDP (Spain 99%, Italy 132.6% and France 96%).

A fiscal union would in effect create a "federal" state for the Eurozone area with calls for its own finance minister (and common budget). Germany sees itself as one of few members running a budget surplus with acceptable levels of public debt/GDP ratio. The long-term permanency of the Euro can only be guaranteed by creating a Eurozone fiscal union that ultimately requires a political one in tandem, which many EU countries openly dislike.

Multi-speed Europe

A key aspect of the discussions for closer integration has focused on a "multi-speed Europe". A group of countries from mainly "Old Europe" (pre-2004 EU accession members) would press ahead with shared policies in particular areas, giving others the opportunity to join later as their economies stabilize. This proposal would lead to a two-speed Europe, a move deeply unpopular with post-2004 accession states whose populist governments continue to lobby for a reduction in Brussels bureaucracy and a return of powers to national governments.

Defence

Most observers argue that deeper integration among Eurozone states is desirable as a means of strengthening monetary union but further consensus is needed. In other matters, such as defence and security, there are proposals for an EU-wide defence policy, but northern and eastern countries see NATO as much more important for their defence. The US administration continues to press for NATO members to meet budget pledges of 2% of GDP—targets that some NATO members are slow to attain.

EU "Soft Power"

The EU can increase its global influence through its soft power for the benefit of its citizens—a role that becomes more imperative at a time of economic (and political) rivalry between the two superpowers, China and the USA. But can this be done on its own especially as the UK will soon be a "third party" country—albeit one closely allied on international terrorism and security matters.

> "There are a number of ways where Europe is stepping up to its role as the main guardian of the international order", said Anthony Gardner, former US Ambassador to the European Union and Senior Adviser at the business advisory firm Brunswick Group and Sidley & Austin, a law firm. He warned, however, that Europe was not able to do the job on its own. "The vacuum cannot be filled by the EU alone, but there is no one else there to fill it. The EU, while doing a very good job, it will struggle ... in the next few years to fill the vacuum", Gardner concluded.[40]

Austria's Permanent Representative to the EU Political and Security Committee, Alexander Kmentt, said the terrain vacated by Washington presented a chance for Europe to step up in areas such as climate change, terrorism and relations with Iran. "The void that is left by the new approach of the United States is an opportunity for Europe. It's a big challenge for us, but I also think that it is a big opportunity", he said. In the current climate, Kmentt argued that the EU had to be flexible in its working arrangements, for example by working with China on climate change even when it disagreed with Beijing on human rights.[41]

European foreign and security policy could also help Europe win back domestic support. "We've lost the economic argument for integration with a large part of our population… foreign and security policy could fill this void with citizens", he acknowledged. "Citizens expect Europe to be a security provider".[42] On foreign policy, Jill Evans MEP would add that …" in a range of conflicts in the Middle East and across the world, the

[40]https://www.euractiv.com/…/europeans-need-a-europe-closer-to-them-says-former-us-….

[41]https://www.icrc.org/en/author/alexander-kmentt.

[42]https://www.friendsofeurope.org/sites/default/files/media-files/soe_report_2018.pdf.

EU could be relied on in helping to keep the peace and emphasize its role in conflict prevention … it is a very influential player on the world stage and should do much more in that sense"[43]

As for the USA, it is still, through NATO, the guarantor of European security, but is critical of Germany's economic ties with Russia over Nord Stream 2 gas supplies, while maintaining sanctions over invasion of Crimea and interference in Ukraine. Signing up to China's Belt and Road Initiative (BRI) under the 16 + 1 has also been criticized by US authorities for allowing Chinese influence in Central and Eastern Europe. At the same time, "America first" trade and security policies provide doubt as to whether the USA can be a reliable ally in the future.

Breaking down market barriers should be part of a wider programme that matches investment in technology, through initiatives like Horizon 2020, with changes in the European regulatory framework to encourage innovation.

"We need to move further to remove still existing barriers to boost growth and innovation. High-tech SMEs create 25% to 50% of the highest paid jobs on the market", Kmentt also said. "In Estonia they create five times more jobs with two times higher salaries compared to traditional companies". Tammist pointed to the development of artificial intelligence (AI) and big data technologies as examples where the EU is slipping further behind due to the disjointed approach of member countries. "We need to avoid the fragmentation of data between the member states. Today there are different regulations covering all aspects of AI and the digital revolution", he added in this vein.[44]

"Harmonisation attempts are underway in the EU, but the digital single market should instead become a data union. Then we could have free movement of data". André Loesekrug-Pietri, Head of the Joint European Disruptive Initiative and a European Young Leader (EYL40), said on the

[43] interview with Jill Evans MEP 5 August 2019.

[44] Ibid.

need to fight fragmentation. “We should get a few policymakers fired”, he argued. “You cannot talk about the digital single market and then encourage fragmentation.

They say they are going to coordinate, but you know this is not going to happen if it is not done from the beginning”.

8 Conclusion

Benefits of membership; Criticism of migration policies; Demands for Change; Recommendations for the Future; Benefits for EU citizens.

The "disintegration" of the EU, Ivan Krastev argues in his book, "After Europe",[1] is not a case of "if", but "when". This is the conclusion he draws from the migrant crisis that broke out in 2015 and which remains one of the existential crises for the EU today. For many—especially East Europeans—Krastev reasons the migrant crisis was a betrayal of the promise of prosperity that accession to the EU originally held out.

The emergence over the past few years of a more confrontational style of politics, in which charismatic leadership matters more than policy and the old division between right and left matters less than that between "internationalists and nativists", leads Krastev to predict that 2017 "may end up being just as consequential" as 1917, the year of the Russian revolution.

[1] Ivan Krastev, University of Pennsylvania Press, 2017.

J. Theodore, *Survival of the European (Dis) Union*,
https://doi.org/10.1007/978-3-030-31214-5_8

But it is hard to reconcile this view with what membership of the EU has delivered for so many of its members—including more recent signatories. Brussels has played a vital role in regenerating the economies of Central and Eastern Europe. Poland and Hungary are the biggest beneficiaries of EU financial largess, drawing in billions of Euros from the EU Structural Funds that are allocated for their countries' regional development.

The EU can claim credit for the enormous benefits in developing its poorer regions through European Regional Development Funds (ERDF) and European Social Funding (ESF), which provide support on a scale that national governments (even in France, Italy or the UK) simply could not afford—or would not, due to their own more partisan priorities. EU Infrastructure projects have built bridges, roads and helped industries grow with billions of euros allocated for research, development and innovation schemes following the Horizon 2020 plan. It is ironic that two of the largest beneficiaries are Hungary and Poland whose "populist" governments are at such odds with the EU today—not only over migration, but also over maintaining the very *democratic* and constitutional principles which each country have signed up to.[2]

However, Brussels can and must take criticism for the manner of its immediate responses to the 2015 migration crises. Little to no account was taken of the particular concerns of those states with broadly ethnically homogeneous populations like Poland and Hungary, who feared immigration would lead to dramatic changes in their nations demographic (and cultural) landscapes. These fears were also held by member states with a more "multicultural" tradition like France, Germany, Italy and Sweden (and the UK pre-Brexit) where problems of integration continue to exist. The delay in action to prevent migration has unnerved governments and fuelled the Eurosceptic agenda. It has provided the focus for the rise of populism throughout Eastern Europe and more recently in Italy and even the UK. It has unleashed opportunist politicians aggressively focused on pushing right-wing anti-democratic agendas at the expense of the established liberal social-democratic order.

Krastev and many others are undoubtedly pessimistic about the consequences of all this. But the fightback has begun. Brussels has taken

[2] https://ec.europa.eu/europe-2020-s.

action to stem the flow of non-EU migrants as part of its flagship strategy.[3] It provides regular reports on progress to prevent *irregular* migration and migrant smuggling along both the Eastern and Central Mediterranean routes and by strengthening the European Border and Coast Guard Agency.[4]

The problem of mass migration has become not just Europe's problem. It has become a major source of tension in US bipartisan politics. What is also forgotten is that countries such as Jordan, Lebanon and Turkey continue to shoulder the main burden of those attempting to migrate to Europe. But Brussels has taken on a new pragmatism (Chapter 3) to combat migration and if successful will defuse much of the raison d'etre for the populist cause.

In the May 2019 European Parliamentary elections while increasing their presence, populist parties have not done quite as well as expected, although the overall turnout by voters went up to 51% of EU electorates. This is in contrast to 42.61% in the previous elections held in 2014 and reflects the rising importance attached to these elections by all sides—liberal-internationalist and populist, left and right, even Europhile and Eurosceptic.[5] However, in the assembled coalition of populist groups/alliances, the parliamentary arithmetic hasn't given populists the majority they hoped for. The pro-European centre that gained new members has essentially held firm in the face of its biggest threat from anti-establishment parties. As the middle ground holds sway—if only just—in the European Parliament, this helps to guarantee the democratic values exemplified by the rule of law constantly challenged by the bloc's leading illiberal democracies. The outgoing EU Commission President, Jean-Claude Junker has reiterated that "Our message to the world is clear and simple: Europe is committed to upholding – and where necessary updating – the rules-based global system. And we are ready to work with everyone to make that happen".[6] This is a clear retort to Vladimir Putin's statement in an FT interview delivered on 27 June on the eve of the Osaka

[3]Chapters 3 and 4.

[4]https://ec.europa.eu/news/management, 4 December 2018.

[5]Over 50% of those eligible to vote took part in the EU Parliamentary elections—the highest turnout in 20 years.

[6]Jean-Claude Junker@JunkerEU (28 June 2019).

G20 conference, in which he argued that "the liberal idea" had "outlived its purpose".[7] Nevertheless, perceptions still remain that a disconnect exists between the political class/elite and ordinary citizens.

The EU was founded on the principle of a supernational entity: one with a common destiny, but claiming to recognize the varying traditions and identities of its members, and that would set the path for a closer economic union within the framework, not of a wholly federated superstructure, but of a partnership between nations. Making the peoples of Europe more prosperous, and avoiding the tragedy of another wholesale European conflict, were foremost in the minds of the founding fathers of the European Economic Community.[8] And this goal can be rightfully claimed as the chief legacy of the founding fathers, with peace reigning in Europe (apart from the Yugoslav civil war) now for 74 years. The former goal—of making its citizens universally more prosperous—has still to be fully realized. As has been argued throughout this book, it is only by doing so that the EU will survive in its current form.

Closer Integration

The project for a more unified Europe, and one progressing towards "closer integration", has come increasingly under attack. When looking through the prism of an increasingly hostile and Eurosceptic electorate, it is hard to see much remaining support for further integration, especially on the political side—outside President Macron's supporting base. This is despite the paradox that an "ever closer union" seems the only way of keeping the Eurozone economically intact.

Analysis, however, bears out that the picture may be more complex than many suppose. For one thing, membership of the European club is still valued by most of the electorates of Europe. Matteo Salvini, the leader of the League in the Italian Coalition, has no intention of an Italian version

---

[7] www.ft.com.

[8] It was never the intention of the founders of the European Economic Community to create a "super state".

of Brexit. For him, as with other Eurosceptics (and, indeed, many British Eurosceptics in the past) fighting the EU from within is seen as the best option.

Lessons of Brexit

So what has been learnt about Brexit? Some would claim it has made a kind of positive impact in mainland Europe. Nobody wants to follow Britain into the political and economic uncertainty it has entered. The paradox is that Brexit has arrested some of the populist movements in Europe, who don't appear to want to put their populations through the process that Britain is presently going through. Marie Le Penn, Salvini, Orban and the Law and Justice Party in Poland have shrunk from some of their extreme positions on the Euro and on the EU. There is a general recognition that politics has to be done on a pan-European basis. In recognition, Salvini travels the EU in search of "populist" alliances to thwart the established liberal–democratic order. But in Britain, we see the creation of a strong pro-EU group in defiant mood to halt a "*no deal*" Brexit.

As bystanders, Europeans have witnessed the unfolding drama that is Brexit and takes no comfort from it—effectively binding the EU together. Populism is seen as much a wake-up call to prompt for EU reform from within—a course advocated by Orban and Salvini.

The Road to Democracy

Those challenging the Brussels' elites advocate the return of decision-making to national Parliaments and the reversal of shared sovereignty, seeing this as having involved the surrender of individual sovereignty for membership of the club. As populist regimes in Italy and Eastern Europe are increasing their representation in the European Parliament, they will be pushing for the repatriation of powers to national parliaments—parliaments determined to eliminate any hope of closer integration.[9]

---

[9] A central issue in the UK Brexit campaign.

There is now a genuine move to make the EU's governing institutions more transparent and democratic to remove the constant criticism of the "democratic deficit". But perceptions of remoteness, bureaucracy and perceived lack of transparency are often criticisms that can be levelled at any "Whitehall" (in London) style state institution—whether, for example, Fonction Publique Francaise (in Paris) and the Deutscher Beamtenbund (in Berlin). In the UK, it goes a step further when criticism by Brexiteers is levelled at the civil service as they scold it for its apparent pro-EU sympathies. It has been accused of thwarting the democratic "will of the people" for its perceived lack of enthusiasm for Brexit and by alerting the government of the dangers of leaving without detailed planning and preparations—and, preferably, with a comprehensive trade agreement in place.

More powers have been given to the directly elected European Parliament: for example, in the approval of recently nominated presidents for the EU Commission. The nominations (including for the President of the ECB) were conducted by the European Council behind closed doors with accusations of a "stitch up", but this is not strictly accurate, as the Council represents the elected Heads of State or of the government of each of the EU27 member states and must be approved by a majority of MEPs (15 July 2019) who have been directly elected by proportional representation in their home states. Ursula von der Leyen (former German Minister of Defence) is now appointed but she can technically be removed, as can the entire EU Commission, if a vote of censure is held by two-thirds of MEPs.

The Parliament now takes the final (democratic) decision with the vote on the President of the Commission and the full Commission for the next five-year term 2019–2024. Finally, the Belgian Prime Minister, Charles Michel, was named as European Council President, taking over from Donald Tusk in November to chair the meetings of EU leaders, with Spain's Josep Borrell leading on foreign policy—a critical role that will need a higher profile for ensuring the EU's relevance as a leading economic power.

But what of democracy in the UK—with Boris Johnson being appointed Prime Minister by a mere 150,000 Conservative party members, a tiny fraction of the voting population? Today Brussels can draw some comfort from a recent poll that puts confidence in the EU at its highest for five years and which confirms 61% of Europeans are optimistic about the future of the EU. The Eurobarometer identifies as many as 55% of Europeans surveyed confirm satisfaction with the way democracy works in the bloc—the highest score since 2004 while support for the euro area reached a record high of 76%.[10]

Critics of the EU Commission always single out a lack of democracy in its operations. It *does* indeed propose new EU laws, but elected MEPs and in the European Council are part of that law-making process. Many initiatives come via national political leaders. These are then deliberated, amended and passed or rejected by the elected representatives of national governments and by directly elected members of the European Parliament.[11] The EU Commission has political leadership functions, as well as its purely administrative ones. As the civil service of a supranational organization, it represents the EU in trade agreements such as CETA, signed with Canada, and the recent successful completion of Free Trade Agreement (FTA) negotiations with Japan and Mercosur (the grouping of Argentina, Brazil Paraguay and Uruguay). The EU is already Mercosur's biggest trade and investment partner, and it's second largest for trade in goods. This could be the most successful EU trade deal—20 years in the making—in terms of reducing tariffs to date, with the savings potentially four times greater than for the trade deals with Canada and Japan combined.[12]

Ignorance of the EU's broad range of duties and functions, including the above, remains almost universal. It has never been in the interests of national governments to promote the ideals and value of EU membership—while it was always ready to accept the benefits of membership. Euro billions have been directed to bolster vital regeneration schemes, such as upgrading transport infrastructure, and projects essential to revitalizing local and regional economies throughout the bloc—especially in Central and Eastern Europe.

But educating Europe's electorates of these successes has not been a priority when governments would rather take the credit for themselves

---

[10]https://www.euronews.com/2019/08/06/trust-in-eu-at-its-highest-in-five-years-new-poll-shows.

[11]MEPs are elected by proportional representation.

[12]http://trade.ec.europa.eu/doclib/press/index.cfm?id=2039.

when things are going right and apportion blame to Brussels when things go wrong. Few school curricula gave prominence to the work of the EU and the functions and role of the EU Commission, its institutions and agencies. At best, only a filtered version of the relevance of its various institutions and on how control is devolved is available to the wider public. But the rise of populists' parties, with their relative recent success, in the European Parliamentary elections helps to bring the EU back to the forefront of citizen's minds.[13] This could very likely provide what President Macron has referred to as a "wakening" call to reinvigorate the European project. Unfortunately, he has few backers for this outside his direct support in France.

What threatens the European project now is not just the aggressive anti-immigration stance of populists like Matteo Salvini of the Italian League, nor is it the breaches of Eurozone budget deficit rules by countries such as Italy and even France that could torpedo efforts to stabilize the currency. Rather, as has been argued earlier, is the increasingly bipolar world driven by economic and geopolitical rivalry between the USA and China, and the question of what position the EU will or should be able to take in this larger set of tensions and struggles. This becomes the overriding challenge facing the new leaders of the EU on taking up their roles in the coming months.[14] What the new leaders must manage is both the simmering crisis of the Eurozone and the cohesion of the EU as a whole. This is best achieved by a delicate balance between the two global power blocks, but with its own position on these matters firmly in mind. It is no longer sufficient to view the EU as a regional economic power—it must use its influence and weight to ensure the protection of the international order, multilateralism and the rule of law beyond its own boundaries. The use of mere soft power is not enough. The EU must take a robust stance against protectionism and the economic costs and political tensions this generates. In doing so, it will achieve the cooperation of China and stand in stark contrast to the protectionist policies of the USA, which are progressively undermining the multilateral approach to international trade. The EU

[13] MEPs sitting in transnational grouping based on political affiliation/ideology.

[14] The new appointments of EU Commission president (Ursula von der Leyen), President of the European Council (Charles Michel) and President of the European Central bank (ECB) Christine Lagarde are to take effect in the autumn of 2019.

should take note that the USA under President Trump has become a less reliable and unstable partner, and as long as this administration lasts, it offers no guarantees to defend liberal democracy in the future.

Demands for Change

EU Commission President Junker's State of the Union address of 12 September 2018 continued the charm offensive delivered in his earlier address in 2016—but now with concrete evidence of growth and improvement in the EU economy, after years of relative stagnation. Junker reaffirmed Europe's position in the world, not only a trade power but also a "global player", and emphasized that "only a strong and united Europe can protect jobs".[15] The Commission recognizes that its success—indeed its very survival—will depend on follow through with realistic proposals on key issues: jobs, migration control, security, together with reforms necessary to improve the functioning of the union and membership of the single currency. Years of austerity, ill-conceived and unpopular refugee policies make this axiomatic for Europe's future political stability. Brussels hopes to put the trauma of Brexit behind it if the UK finally leaves, as promised, on 31 October 2019. It can now get on with the business of meeting the expectations of citizens of the EU27 in those matters of vital concern. It will not alter the drivers of migration in the future, but it can and has already started to implement better processes for facilitating the return home of economic migrants and those refused asylum. Aid packages in particular for countries in Africa, coupled with local onsite processing centres, will support a more proactive immigration policy. Bolstering security on the borders of Europe with the expansion of Frontex will help to meet the demands of EU citizens critical of "open borders" under lax Schengen arrangements. On this, the EU has gone a step further with the deployment of its border protection agency to Albania to support police there

[15] https://europa.eu/rapid/press-release_SPEECH-18-5808.

in stopping illegal immigration. This is Frontex's first mission outside EU territory, with Brussels calling it a "game changer".[16]

With the creation of the Eurozone from 1999 and the enlargement of the EU since 2004, it has become even more important to explain its importance to EU citizens. Rejecting the status quo, however, falls short of member states questioning their support for the Union per se. Renewing confidence in the Eurozone is the challenge for both the EU Commission and the ECB. But how is this to be achieved?

The European Council has nominated a new ECB President, Christine Lagarde, to replace the outgoing President Mario Draghi. She is not an economist, but has served for two years as minister of trade and four years as minister for economy and finance in the governments of French Presidents Jacques Chirac and Nicolas Sarkozy. Then, for the past eight years, she has been managing director of the International Monetary Fund. Although Lagarde has trained as a lawyer, she may be uniquely qualified to lead the ECB as it manages monetary policy in the Eurozone and addresses the challenges emanating from the global economy. New strategies to Eurozone reform may need to be applied, recognizing a more flexible approach. An agreement should allow the introduction of counter-cyclical policies to help ameliorate the process of boom and bust that plagued the Eurozone through the twenty-first century up to the debt crisis of 2010–2012.[17] Populists and Eurosceptics know that national governments are incapable, by virtue of Euro membership, of devaluing their currencies, but a new way of handling fiscal policy is required: this will require fiscal union as the default, a common Eurozone budget, and fiscal transfers to the poorer Eurozone members-sharing sovereignty as an alternative to manage the problems created through the barriers to independent fiscal policy.

---

[16]https://www.dw.com/en/eus-frontex-border-force-deploys-teams-to-albania-to-halt-migrants/a-48823658.

[17]In a recession, Eurozone members should be allowed to spend more to help counter the downturn and rein in spending when the economy is doing better.

Recommendations for the Future

As we have discussed, the debt crisis has shown that some level of fiscal integration and debt mutualization is likely the only way for the Eurozone to ultimately survive. Eurozone leaders are finding it more difficult with each bailout rescue to balance their economic decisions with the political implications they create. Economists have long been familiar with a concept known as "moral hazard"—a scenario which creates incentive for individuals to act recklessly by insulating them from the consequences of their actions. By insuring risk, governments create perverse incentives that make banks less cautious and less willing to appropriately price such risk. In the case of the Eurozone, instead of the banks making effective provisions in the event of financial trouble, the government assured cheap credit, backed as it was by both low interest rates and the supportive financial structure of the EU and then the Eurozone. But the nature of the bailouts, which shifted the burden of reckless lending away from the banks and onto the vulnerable economies of the EU, gave the implications of moral hazard a whole new dimension and has burned through much of the popular faith in the common European project.

The new members of Central and Eastern Europe have embraced the principle of free movement for EU citizens and have for the most part been the main beneficiaries of it—having migrated in large numbers to the UK, Germany and other North-West richer states for higher paid jobs and better living standards. But sharing these privileges (which they pay for in their contributions to the EU budget) with non-EU migrants from Syria, Iraq, Afghanistan and other Muslim countries is quite another matter. Germany's EU neighbours such as Poland, Hungary, the Czech Republic and Slovakia in the Visegrad group still resist by not subscribing to the Brussels relocation quota scheme. Instead, they sit in harmony with Matteo Salvini's Eurosceptic Italian coalition, taking a tough line and continue to vehemently oppose refugee policies and uncontrolled migration.

Angela Merkel had in late 2016 soon after the UK referendum described the European Union to be at a critical juncture. She had arrived in Bratislava for a special summit—without the UK—that hoped to set a new course for a project battered by Brexit. "We have to show with our actions that we can get better", the German chancellor said. The bloc had to improve "in the domain of security, internal and external security, the fight against terrorism, the cooperation in the field of defence", as well as defence and jobs, she added.[18] Today the newly appointed European Commission President, Ursula von der Leyen, has pledged an ambitious programme which helped to secure her appointment by the European Parliament.[19] To please the Green and liberal caucus, she included a new EU carbon border tax, carbon neutrality by 2050 in stating "I want Europe to become the first climate neutral continent in the world by 2050".[20] She has promised to get tough with the international tech giants who "play" the European tax system, thus following in the footsteps of Margrethe Vestager the Danish EU Competition Commissioner. All these were presented in a 24-page "policy framework" that championed environmental issues, social policies and gender equality.

Benefits for EU Citizens

Democracy, human rights and the rule of law are entrenched as fundamental benefits. But these alone don't set the EU apart—as many of Europe's democracies have these built into their legal fabric to a greater or lesser extent. However, Brussels has continued to legislate on a range of citizens' rights relating particularly to consumer and employment rights.[21]

Brussels continues to lead the way on improving all EU citizens' rights in its reforms on data protection—in particular, in its most recent reforms in May 2018 on EU data protection rules. These give citizens more control over their personal data and benefits businesses with a level playing field. A recent case involving British Airways arose where the airline was fined £183m by the UK data regulator after hackers stole information from

[18] https://www.theguardian.com/world/2016/sep/16/bratislava-summit-donald-tusk-urges-eu-leaders-not-to-waste-brexit-crisis?

[19] Ursula von der Leyen secured approval with 383 votes—only 9 more than needed to secure the EU Parliamentary majority.

[20] Statement by Ursula von der Leyen on her confirmation as President of the EU Commission by the EU Parliament, 16 July 2019.

[21] https://europa.eu/european-union/about-eu/what-the-eu-does-for-its-citizens_en.

more than 500,000 customers. This related to breaching European data rules after the company's Web site and mobile app were hacked in 2018. It is the first significant penalty to be imposed on a company after the introduction of Europe-wide data protection rules and sends a warning on the importance of shielding customer data from hackers.

The facts of the case were that data had been compromised by poor security, which included highly confidential login and card payment details, bookings and addresses. Elizabeth Denham, the UK Information Commissioner, stated that: "When you are entrusted with personal data you must look after it. Those that don't will face scrutiny from my office to check they have taken appropriate steps to protect fundamental privacy rights".[22]

The expansion of the EU itself in the 2000s, in the context of the weak macroeconomic picture since the Great Recession, has been riven with political consequences and a huge spur to the opposition to open immigration policies now seen in Britain as elsewhere in Europe culminating in Brexit. Even if the arguments against the East European expansion rest on valid economic reasoning, the very nature and purpose of the EU—as a unifying economic, social and political collaborative project—rendered the expansion inevitable. Joining the EU has offered both the former dictatorships of the Mediterranean littoral and Eastern Europe's former communist satellites admission to the democratic club of "old" Europe, and for this, they and the world should be thankful. The EU has been instrumental in gaining them recognition as parliamentary democracies based on the rule of law—with the added bonus of funding the growth and expansion of their fledging economies.

How could financial assistance be refused when there was no dispute that they were significantly poorer than the Northern EU countries? The author here argues in favour of the overall process of Eastern EU enlargement, despite the potential problems that have arisen as a result.

With the benefit of hindsight, was the entire EU expansion to the East a mistake? No. If the East was to be brought in from the economic cold, living standards could be raised and their economies would come to be less reliant on Moscow. There *were* obvious difficulties in integrating eleven

[22]www.ft.com.

new countries, with a population exceeding 100 million, and a political culture, history and economic condition far different to their western neighbours. But then again, is this not what the EU is all about? And were there not cultural differences and different political histories among the old EU-15? It is true that five out of the original six EEC countries (France, West Germany, Belgium, the Luxemburg and the Netherlands) together with the UK, Ireland and Denmark that joined the European Economic Community in 1973 share a similar political background and history based on parliamentary democracies since the end of the Second World War. But the enlargement of the East had echoes of the Mediterranean enlargement of the 1980s—when Greece joined in 1981, followed by Spain and Portugal in 1986—that integrated almost 60 million more people into the EEC, many of whom had lived in the shadows of monarchy, fascism or dictatorial rule. Similar fears about mass migration or the economic "drag" of those nations were raised at the time. But that integration was broadly successful, at least until the Euro crisis almost thirty years later.

Even if the arguments against the East European expansion rest on valid economic reasoning, the very nature of the EU rendered the expansion inevitable. Joining the EU offered "new Europe" not only funds from EU institutions, but, above all, it helped consolidate the rule of law based on democratic processes irrespective of (illiberal) tendencies surfacing recently in Hungary and Poland dealt with in Chapter 5.

It is inconceivable that *for example* Germany would reject integrating these new countries to the EU, when it had to undergo—at great economic cost to the former Federal Republic of Germany—its own process of integrating the DDR (East Germany) as part of German re-unification in the early 1990s?

The ongoing crisis, of which Brexit is the latest and most novel manifestation, exposes a deep contradiction at the heart of Europe—between the Eurozone's need for successful integration and voters' (and protestors') overwhelming rejection of it. If such populism continues to rise, it would not be a large leap from here for a member of the single currency to win a democratic mandate to quit it altogether—a Lehman-like event which would not only reignite the worst of the crisis, but also put the survival of the entire European project in the balance. Political upsets can be much harder to put to rights than economic ones, and it would not take much to bring another party like Syriza to power or at least hold the balance of power—as was feared in the snap presidential election in Greece in December 2014, which sent markets tumbling.[23] Nor would it take much now to elect a Brexit-emboldened, largely anti-EU right-wing party such as the National Rally party in France (formerly the National Front until June 2018)—or its rising equivalents in Hungary and Poland. The guiding principle for the EU Commission is increasingly for closer union to be off the table.

Although there is substantial criticism of the EU in Eastern Europe, overall sentiment is quite different, with all major polls showing a substantial majority in favour of remaining.

Brussels can, and must, take criticism for the manner of its immediate response to the 2015 migration crisis and for the long and sometimes brutal austerity approach to tackling to Eurozone debt crises since 2012. The battle to save the Euro has also led to an unprecedented centralization of authority over banking, budgets and welfare and further stocked populist tensions in the bloc.

At the same time, however, the EU can claim credit for the enormous benefits it has delivered in developing its poorer regions and the impact of its infrastructure and investment projects across Europe. Ignorance of the EU's broad range of duties and functions in this regard remains almost universal—and national governments enjoy taking credit for its achievements when things go right and blaming Brussels when they go wrong.

Ultimately, the chief threat to the European project is not simply the rise of regional populism or the failings within the Eurozone, but the increasingly multipolar world driven by the rising superpower rivalry of the USA and China, and the question of how the EU starts to position itself within this unfolding political/economic conflict. EU member states have good reason to stay under the EU economic umbrella. In world trade terms, their small economies are not able to negotiate *on a level playing field* with either the USA or China, a fact the UK will soon learn when attempting to trade solo under the mantra of "Global Britain". The drama

[23] http://www.ft.com/cms/s/0/4db45c9c-7f95-11e4-b4f5-00144feabdc0.html#axzz3Lxt5XLDc.

playing out in the current US–China trade tariff war is stark evidence of this. Bilateral transactional deals are the focus of US economic policy in keeping with the slogan of "America first". This was very much the case when the US enforced a renegotiation of the NAFTA (The North American Free Trade Agreement) with its partners, Canada and Mexico in 2018.

After China, the Trump administration has its sights on the EU particularly as it sees the EU as one of the main beneficiaries of *its* tariff war with China.[24] The EU may well have support from China for the preservation of WTO rules and the global world order, but politically and militarily its allegiance has to gravitate towards the USA (and NATO) despite volatility in relations today.

[24] https://www.atlanticcouncil.org/blogs/new-atlanticist/after-china-will-the-eu-be-the-next-target-of-trump-s-tariffs.

Bibliography

Bannerman, C. D. MEP. (2016). *Time To Jump: A Positive Vision of a Britain Out of the EU and in EEA Life*. Epsom, UK: Bretwalda Books.

Barnes. T. (2018). 'Italy Slashes Retirement Age and Launches Citizen's Income' https://www.independent.co.uk/news/world/europe/italy-budget-basic-income-retirement-age-lowered-tax-cuts-spending-five-star-league-a8704081.html.

BBC. (2016a). 'China's Economic Slowdown Deepens' http://www.bbc.com/news/business/economy, downloaded 14 August 2016.

BBC. (2016b). 'Italian Economy Stagnates as German Growth Slows' http://www.bbc.com/news/business-37056800, downloaded 12 August 2016.

Bongardt, A., & Torres, F. (2016). 'The Political Economy of Brexit: Why Making It Easier to Leave the Club Could Improve the EU' *Inter-economics*, 51 (4), 214–219.

Bongiovanni, Francesco M. (2018). *Europe and the End of the Age of Innocence*. Cham: Palgrave Macmillan.

Brooks, R. (2016). *The Great Tax Robbery*. London, UK: One World Publications.

Brush, S., & Weber, A. (2019). 'Brexit Breakthrough Reached on Finance, Helping Avert No-Deal Rupture' Bloomberg, https://www.bloomberg.com/news/articles/2019-02-01/brexit-breakthrough-reached-on-finance-to-avert-no-deal-rupture?srnd=premium-europe, downloaded 1 February 2019.

J. Theodore, *Survival of the European (Dis) Union*,
https://doi.org/10.1007/978-3-030-31214-5

Bulmer, Simon, & Paterson, William. (2018). *Germany and the European Union: Europe's Reluctant Hegemon.* London, UK: Macmillan Education.

Campbell, P., & Tetlow, G. (2016). 'Indian Business Welcomes UK Trade Deal' FT, http://www.ft.com/cms/s/0/2e0eb278-4372-11e6-b22f-79eb4891c97d.html#axzz4FpTCFbuR, downloaded 30 July 2016.

Cassell, M., & Hutcheson, A. (2019). 'Explaining Germany's Position on European Banking Union' *German Politics* published online 29 May 2019: https://www.tandfonline.com/doi/abs/10.1080/09644008.2019.1621296?journalCode=fgrp20.

Centre for Economic Policy Research. (2015). 'Rebooting the Eurozone: Step I –Agreeing a Crisis Narrative' Policy Insight No. 85.

Centre of Economic Policy Research. (2018). 'Reconciling Risk Sharing with Market Discipline: A Constructive Approach to Euro Area Reform' Policy Insight No. 91.

Connelly, Tony. (2017). *Brexit & Ireland—He Dangers. The Opportunities, and the Inside Story of the Irish Response.* London: Penguin Books.

Costigan, T., Cottle, D., & Keys, A. (2017). 'The US Dollar as the Global Reserve Currency: Implications for Us Hegemony' *World Review of Political Economy,* 8 (1), 104–122.

Dakers, M. (2019). 'U.K. Projects Face Multi-Billion Pound Funding Gap When Brexit Cuts Off EIB' Bloomberg, https://www.bloomberg.com/news/articles/2019-01-31/british-projects-face-funding-shortfall-as-brexit-cuts-off-eib, downloaded 31 January 2019.

De Grauwe, P. (2016). 'European Monetary Unification: A Few Lessons for East Asia' *Scottish Journal of Political Economy,* 63 (1), 7–17.

De Grauwe, P. (2018). *Economics of Monetary Union* (12th ed.). Oxford: Oxford University Press.

De Grauwe, P., & Ji, Y. (2016). 'How to Reboot the Eurozone and Ensure Its Long-Term Survival' CEPR's Policy Portal, https://voxeu.org/article/how-reboot-eurozone-and-ensure-its-long-term-survival.

Dendrinou, V. (2018). 'EU Takes on Dollar's Global Dominance in New Push for the Euro' Bloomberg, https://www.bloomberg.com/news/articles/2018-12-05/eu-takes-on-dollar-s-global-dominance-in-new-push-for-euro?srnd=premium-europe, downloaded 5 December 2018.

Dmitracova, O. (2019). 'Bank of England's Carney Sees Clouds on the Horizon for UK Consumers' https://www.independent.co.uk/news/business/news/bank-of-england-carney-slow-pay-growth-uk-consumers-a8975846.html.

Dreyer, O., & Gerlach, S. (2016). 'Germany's Idiosyncratic Views Test Cohesion of Eurozone' 12/05, FT.

Duke, S. (2016). 'Europe's Attack on Google Is the Latest Skirmish in a High-stakes Battle with America's Technology Titans' 24/04, *The Sunday Times.*
Editorial. (2016). 'China's Biggest Economic Challenge' Bloomberg, https://www.bloomberg.com/view/articles/2016-08-25/china-s-biggest-economicchallenge, downloaded 26 August 2016.
Efstathiou, K., & Papadia, F. (2018). 'The International Role of the Euro' Bruegel, http://bruegel.org/2018/12/the-international-role-of-the-euro/.
Eichengreen, B. Wyplotz. (2016). 'Minimal Conditions for the Survival of the Euro' *Inter-economics,* 51(1), 24–28, https://doi.org/10.1007/s10272-016-0569-z.
Eijffinger, S., & De Haan, J. (2002). 'European Monetary and Fiscal Policy' Europa, http://eur-lex.europa.eu/summary/chapter/taxation/2101.html?root=2101, downloaded 12 August 2016.
Euro Area Countries' http://www.bruegel.org/nc/blog/detail/article/1151-15-percent-to-plus-4-percent-taylor-rule-interest-rates-for-euro-area-countries, downloaded 25 April 2016.
European Commission. (2015). 'The Five Presidents' Report: Completing Europe's Economic and Monetary Union'.
European Commission. (2017a). 'Reflection Paper on the deepening of the Economic and Monetary Union' Paper 291, https://ec.europa.eu/commission/publications/reflection-paper-deepening-economic-and-monetary-union_en.
European Commission. (2017b). 'White Paper on the Future of Europe: Reflections and Scenarios for the EU27 By 2025'.
European Commission. (2018). 'State of the Union 2018: By Jean-Claude Juncker, President of the European Commission' https://ec.europa.eu/commission/sites/beta-political/files/soteu2018-brochure_en.pdf, downloaded 12 September 2018.
European Commission, Statistics. (2016). http://trade.ec.europa.eu/doclib/docs/2006/september/tradoc_113366.pdf, downloaded 31 July 2016.
Eurostat. (2003). *Fifty Year of Statistics on Europe.* Luxemburg: Office for Official Publications.
Evans, P. A. (2016). 'Italy Much Choose Between the Euro and Its Own Economic Survival', *The Telegraph,* http://www.telegraph.co.uk/business/2016/05/11/italy-must-chose-between.
Flassbeck, H., & Lapavitsas, C. (2015). *Against the Troika Crisis and Austerity in the Eurozone.* London, UK: Verso.
Glover, J., & Sirletti, S. (2016). 'Monte Paschi Capital Wiped Out in European Bank Stress Test' downloaded 30 July 2016.

Gourinchas, P. O. (2017). 'The Fundamental Structure of the International Monetary System' In Bordo, M. and Taylor, J. (Eds.), *Rules for International Monetary Stability: Past, Present and Future*. Stanford: Hoover Institution Press Publication, pp. 169–185.

Grice, A. (2019). 'Theresa May Is Banking on the EU to Save Her Deal—But a Distracted Europe has Bigger Fish to Fry' https://www.independent.co.uk/voices/brexit-theresa-may-backstop-northern-ireland-eu-jean-claude-juncker-a8711206.html, downloaded 5 January 2019 .

Hinarejos, A. (2013). 'Fiscal Federalism in the European Union: Evolution and Future Choices for EMU' *Common Market Law Review*, 50, 1621–1642.

Horta, S. (2016). 'Europe's Tumbling Lenders Lose Almost Half Their Value in a Year' Bloomberg, http://www.bloomberg.com/news/articles/2016-08-02/europe-s-tumbling-lenders-lose-almost-half-their-value-in-a-year, downloaded 2 August 2016.

Hutton, Will, & Adonis, Andrew. (2018). *Saving Britain*. London: Abacus.

IMF. (2016). 'Currency Composition of Official Foreign Exchange Reserves' COFER, http://data.imf.org/?sk=E6A5F467-C14B-4AA8-9F6D-5A09EC4E62A4&sId=1408202905739, downloaded 31 July 2016.

International Monetary Fund. (2018a). 'Currency Composition of Official Foreign Exchange Reserves' http://data.imf.org/?sk=E6A5F467-C14B-4AA8-9F6D-5A09EC4E62A4.

International Monetary Fund. (2018b). 'Special Drawing Right' https://www.imf.org/en/About/Factsheets/Sheets/2016/08/01/14/51/Special-Drawing-Right-SDR.

Karagounis, K., Syrrakos, D., & Simister, J. (2015). 'The Stability and Growth Pact, Rand Balanced Budget Fiscal Stimulus: Evidence from Germany and Italy' *Inter-economics*, 50 (1), 32–39.

Kearns, Ian. (2018). *Collapse—Europe After the European Union*. La Vergne: Biteback Publishing.

Klein, C. M. (2016). 'What If Greece Got Massive Debt Relief But No One Admitted It?' (Part-2), FT.

Krastev, Ivan. (2017). *After Europe*. Philadelphia: University of Pennsylvania Press.

Krugman, P. (2012). 'Crash of the Bumblebee' *The New York Times*, 29 July 2012: A19.

Lapavitsas et al. (2012). *Crisis in the Eurozone*. London, UK: Verso.

Lavoie, M. (2015b). 'The Eurozone Crisis: A Balance-of-Payments Problem or a Crisis Due to a Flawed Monetary Design?' *International Journal of Political Economy*, 44 (2), 157–160.

Less Theodore, J., Theodore, J., & Dimitrios, S. (2017). *The European Union and the Eurozone Under Stress: Challenges and Solutions for Re-pairing Fault Lines in the European Project.* Manchester: Palgrave Macmillan.

Lucarelli, B. (2012). 'German Neomercantilism and the European Sovereign Debt Crisis' *Journal of Post-Keynesian Economics,* 34 (2), 205–224.

Marsh, D. (2011). *The Euro: The Battle for the New Global Currency.* Yale, USA: Yale University Press.

Marsh, D. (2013). *Europe's Deadlock: How the Euro Crisis Could be Solved—And Why It Won't Happen.* Yale, USA: Yale University Press.

Mazower, M. (2016). 'Berlin Should Be Careful What It Wishes for' FT.

McKinsey Report. (2015). *The Future of the Euro, An Economic Perspective on the Eurozone Crisis.* Germany: McKinsey & Company, Inc.

Munchau, W. (2019). 'Threats to European Integration Are Growing' *Financial Times,* Monday 12 August 2019, p. 2.

Murray, B. (2018). 'Dollar Share of Currency Reserves Slips to Near Five-Year Low' Bloomberg, https://www.bloomberg.com/news/articles/2018-12-28/dollar-share-of-currency-reserves-slips-to-near-five-year-low?srnd=premium-europe; http://dx.doi.org/10.1080/09692290.2012.644509, downloaded 30 December 2018.

Murray, Douglas. (2017). *The Strange Death of Europe.* London: Bloomsbury.

Noel, M. Sir. (2016). 'EU Goes Far Beyond the Normal Nature of a Treaty Organisation' 06/05, FT.

Pancevki, B., & Campbell, M. (2016). 'Migrants March into Storm of Hatred' 25/10, *The Sunday Times.*

Peet, J., & Guardia, A. L. (2014). 'Unhappy Union—How the Euro Crisi-and Europe-Can Be Fixed' *Economist Newspaper.*

Quaglia, L. (2019). 'The Politics of an "Incomplete" Banking Union and Its "Asymmetric" Effects' *Journal of European Integration* published online 27 May 2019: https://www.tandfonline.com/doi/abs/10.1080/07036337.2019.1622541?journalCode=geui20.

Reganti, A. (2016). *The Reserve: The Dollar, the Renminbi and Status of Reserve.* New York: GMO White Paper.

Research on Money and Finance. (2011). 'Breaking Up? A Route out of the Eurozone Crisis', Lapavitsas, C., Kaltenbrunner, A., Lindo, D., Meadway, J., Michell, J., Panceira, J. P., Pires, E., Powell, J., Stenfors, A., Teles, N., Vatikiotis, V., RMF Occasional Report 3, November, 2011.

Rhodes, W. (2016). 'Eurozone Must Complete Banking Union to Avert Crisis' http://www.ft.com/cms/s/0/5eb51992-5413-11e6-9664-e0bdc13c3bef.html#axzz4FpTCFbuR, downloaded 30 July 2016.

Robinson, E. (2016). 'Italian Banks Reel But Monti Has No Regrets for Avoiding Bailout' http://www.bloomberg.com/news/articles/2016-08-09/italian-banksreel-but-monti-has-no-regrets-for-avoiding-bailout, downloaded 10 August 2016.

Ryan, C. (2016). 'Brexit Sees UK Consumer Confidence Fall Most Since 1990' http://www.bloomberg.com/news/articles/2016-07-28/brexit-sends-u-kconsumer-confidence-falling-most-since-1990, downloaded 30 July 2017.

Sandbu, M. (2016). 'Italy Fears Brexit Would Damage Whole of Europe' 19/04, FT.

Sanderson, R. (2016). 'Monte dei Paschi Board Backs Private Sector Rescue Plan' FT, http://www.ft.com/cms/s/0/1d47b04a-5586-11e6-9664-e0bdc13c3bef.html#axzz4FpTCFbuR, downloaded 30 July 2016.

Sibert, A. (2010). 'The EFSM and the EFSF: Now and What Follows' Directorate General for Internal Policies, Policy Department A: Economic and Scientific Policies, Economic and Monetary Affairs.

Simitis, C. (2014). *The European Debt Crisis.* Manchester, UK: Manchester University Press.

Sladkowska, B., & Strzelecki. (2016). 'More Poles Are Now Moving to Germany than the U.K.' Bloomberg, http://www.bloomberg.com/news/articles/2016-09-18/more-poles-are-now-moving-to-germany-than-the-u-k, downloaded 18 September 2016.

Stiglitz, Joseph E. (2016). *The Euro—And Its Threat to the Future of Europe.* London: Penguin.

Syrrakos, D. (2016). 'The Franco-German Alliance and Its Role in the Process of European Monetary Integration. 1944–2010' *Olsztyn Economic Journal,* 11 (2), 119–135.

Syrrakos, D. (2017). 'Economic Impact and Manufacturing' In Tse, H. (Ed.), *Doing Business After Brexit: A Practical Guide to Legal Challenges* (1st ed.). London, UK: Bloomsbury Professional. https://www.bloomsburyprofessional.com//uk/doing-business-after-brexit-9781784519360/.

Syrrakos, D. (2018). 'Greece Exits Its Third Bailout—But Eurozone Still Has Much to Learn from the Crisis' *The Conversation,* http://theconversation.com/greece-exits-its-third-bailout-but-eurozone-still-has-much-to-learn-from-the-crisis-101709, downloaded August 2018.

Theodore, John, Theodore, Jonathan, with Syrrakos, Dimitrios. (2017). *The European Union and the Eurozone Under Stress.* Basingstoke: Palgrave Macmillan. https://www.bbc.co.uk/news/business-46377309.

Treanir, J. (2018). 'Bank Warns No-Deal Could See UK Sink into Recession'.

Varoufakis, Yanis. (2016). *And The Weak Suffer What They Must?* New York: Nation Books.

Vaughan-Williams, N. (2015). *Europe's Boarder Crisis: Bio-Political Security and Beyond.* Oxford University Press. https://www.europarl.europa.eu/resources/library/media/20190716RES57231/20190716RES57231.pdf.

Wilding, Peter (2017). *What Next?—Britain's Future in Europe.* London: I.B. Tauris.

Wyplosz, C. (2014). 'The Eurozone Crisis: A Near-Perfect Case of Mismanagement' *Journal of Applied Economics,* XXXIII (1): 1–13.

Yang, B. Z., & Zeng, T. (2014). 'A Note on the Real Currency Exchange Rate: Definitions and Implications' *Journal of International Business and Economics,* 2 (4), 45–55.

Index

A

'America first' 76, 106, 146, 164
Austerity 1, 2, 4, 26–28, 51, 67, 74, 81, 127, 128, 140, 141, 157, 163
Autocratic 68, 71, 89, 90, 100, 131

B

Banking crisis 31, 33
Banking union 34–36, 45
'Brussels Effect' 136, 137
Budget deficit 29, 30, 109, 143, 144, 156

C

Capital markets union (CMU) 12, 35–37
Closer integration 6, 144, 152, 153

D

Democratic values 14, 19, 68, 85, 151
(Weaponizing) the dollar 23, 38–41, 43, 122, 123

E

EU Mobility 47
European deposit insurance scheme (EDIS) 35
European monetary system 43
European Monetary Union (EMU) 25, 26
European Regional Development Fund (ERDF) 8, 99, 150
Euroscepticism 128
Existential threat 59

J. Theodore, *Survival of the European (Dis) Union*,
https://doi.org/10.1007/978-3-030-31214-5

F

Fiscal rules 45, 46
Freedom of movement (FOM) 48, 50, 52, 53, 56, 62, 75, 92, 97
Free Trade Agreement (FTA) 9, 14, 115, 135, 136, 155, 164
Frontex 61, 63, 157, 158

G

Global 1, 2, 12, 14, 16, 19, 23, 26, 27, 37–42, 60, 66, 69, 74–78, 97, 105, 106, 109, 113, 114, 117–119, 123, 132, 135–138, 141, 145, 149, 151, 156, 158, 164
Globalization 2
Global player/role 12, 123, 135, 157
Gross domestic product (GDP) 14, 26, 27, 29–31, 36, 43–45, 99, 109, 143, 144

I

Identity politics 4, 78, 79
Illiberal democracies 9, 79, 89, 151
Instrument in Support of Trade Exchanges (INSTEX) 40
International trade 39, 43, 45, 82, 119, 120, 156

L

Liberal democracy 1, 20, 90, 91, 157
Liberal values 85, 90, 94

M

Migration 11, 12, 14, 16, 18, 34, 47–52, 58, 59, 62, 65–71, 74, 81, 87, 90–92, 111, 123, 126, 127, 130, 149–151, 157, 159, 162, 163
Multiculturalism 88, 127
Multilateralism 37, 39, 105, 156

N

Nativism 76, 78, 91, 93
No deal (Brexit) 2, 4, 7, 10, 13, 18, 20, 21, 23, 30, 36, 49, 52, 54, 55, 59, 60, 63, 73, 79–81, 83, 84, 88, 112, 120, 122, 123, 125, 128, 133, 134, 136, 139, 141, 142, 153, 154, 157, 159, 161, 162
Non Performing Loans (NPLs) 32, 45

O

Open borders 63, 88, 157

P

Populism 16, 21, 34, 59, 62, 73, 74, 76–78, 81, 85, 88, 91, 101, 126, 150, 153, 162, 163

Q

Quantitative Easing (QE) 26, 31, 34, 43–45

R

Refugee quotas 58, 61, 66, 100
Reserve currency 23, 36, 41, 107, 122, 123

S
Schengen 12, 49, 63–65, 74, 82, 92, 127, 157
Soft power 145, 156
Strategic Agenda 11, 12, 15, 97, 105, 123
Structural funds 8, 81, 99, 130, 150
Superstate 133

T
Threats 4, 12, 21, 23, 30, 34, 38, 39, 50, 59, 62, 67, 69, 76, 113, 118, 127, 128, 131, 151, 163

9783030312138